33 CLASSIC HITS FOR EASY PIANO

DISCARD

ISBN 0-7935-9346-8

HAL•LEONARD®
CORPORATION
7777 W. BLUEMOUND RD. P.O. BOX 13819 MILWAUKEE, WI 53213

Visit Hal Leonard Online at
www.halleonard.com

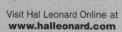

ALL BY MYSELF

Music by SERGEI RACHMANINOFF
Words and Additional Music by ERIC CARMEN

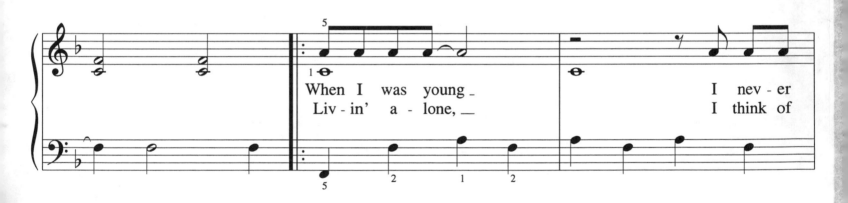

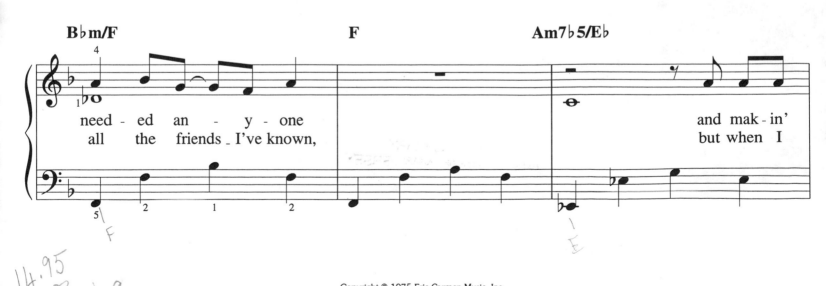

love was just ___ for fun;
dial the tel - e - phone

those days ___ are gone.
no - bod - y's home.

All by ___ my - self, ___

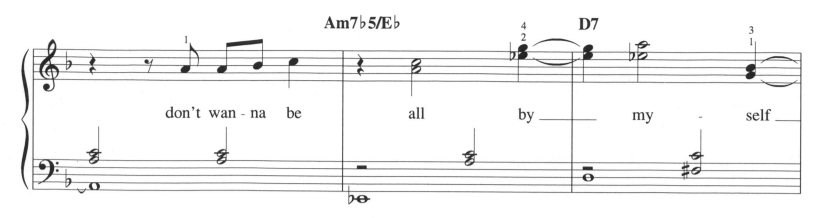

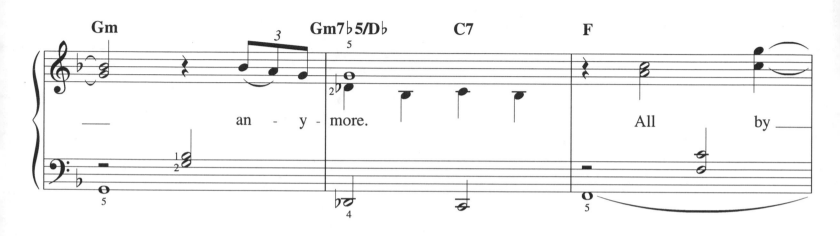

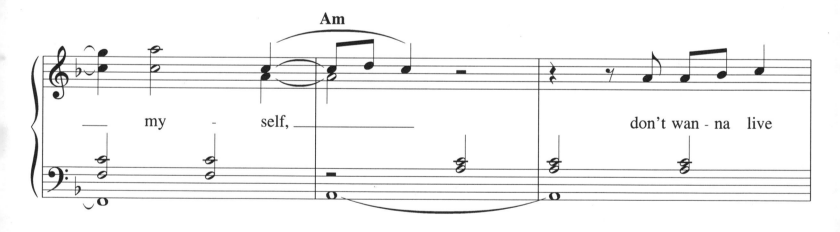

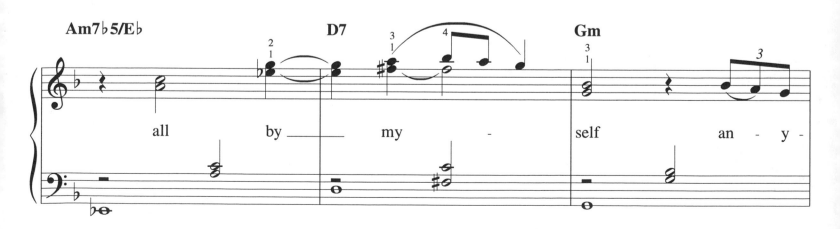

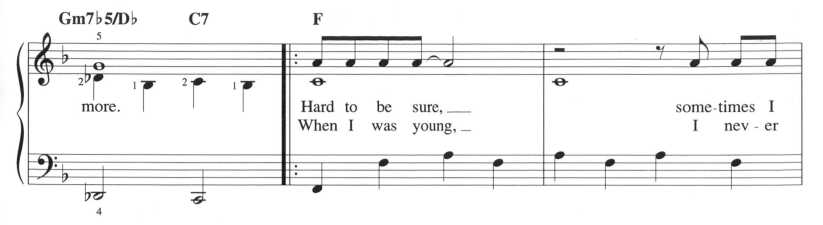

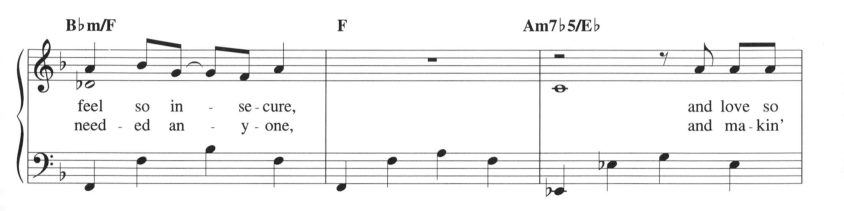

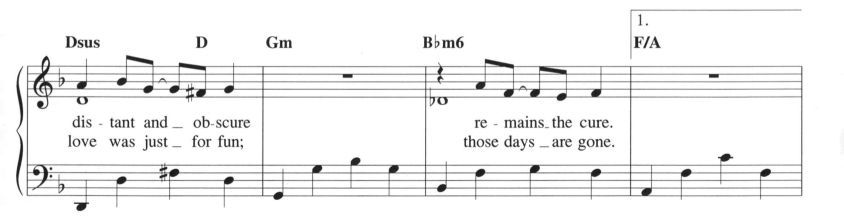

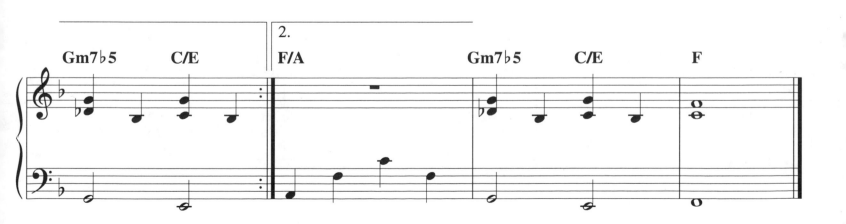

ALWAYS

Words and Music by
JON BON JOVI

Slow rock ballad

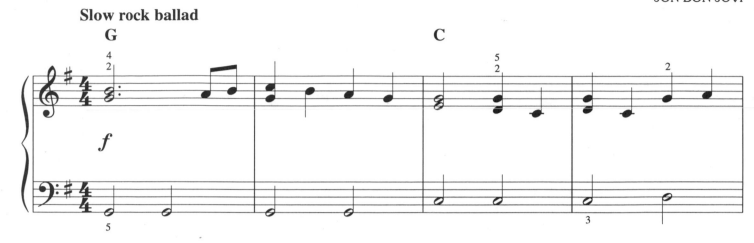

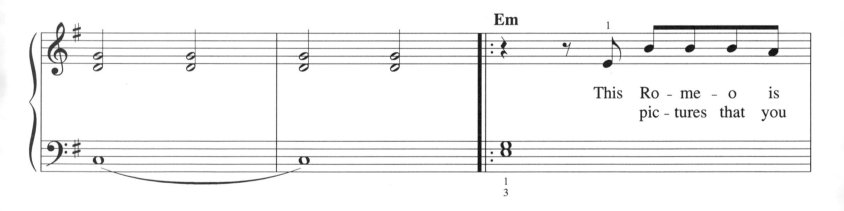

This Ro - me - o   is
pic - tures that you

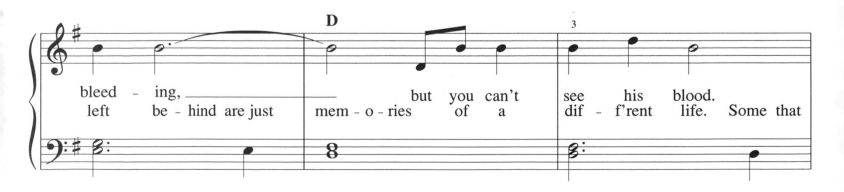

bleed - ing, _____ but you can't   see his blood.
left be - hind are just mem - o - ries of a dif - f'rent life. Some that

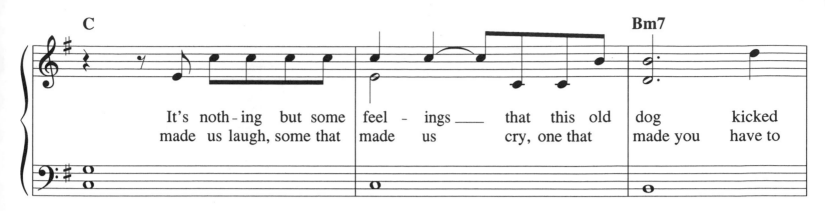

It's noth - ing but some feel - ings ___ that this old dog kicked
made us laugh, some that made us cry, one that made you have to

up.
say good - bye. What I'd

It's been rain - ing since you left me, now I'm
give to run my fin - gers through your hair, to

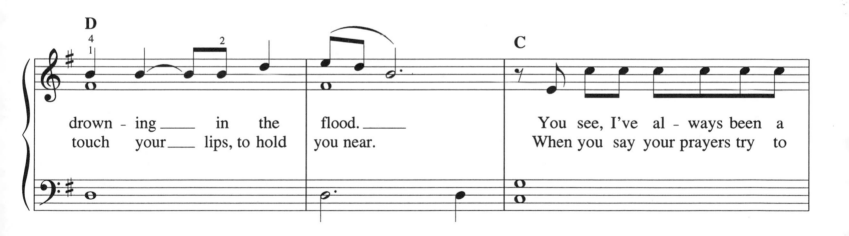

drown - ing ___ in the flood. ___
touch your ___ lips, to hold you near.

You see, I've al - ways been a
When you say your prayers try to

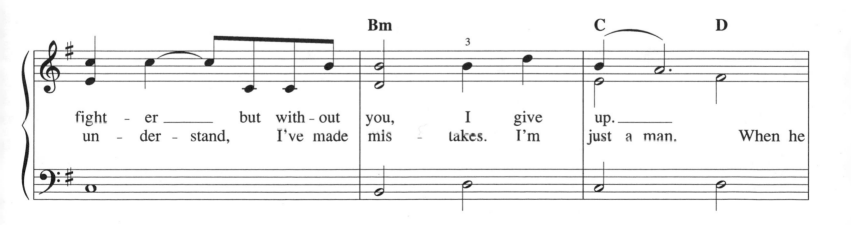

fight - er ___ but with - out you, I give up. ___
un - der - stand, I've made mis - takes. I'm just a man. When he

Now I can't sing a | love song | like the | way it's meant to
holds you close, when he | pulls you near, | when he | says the words you've been

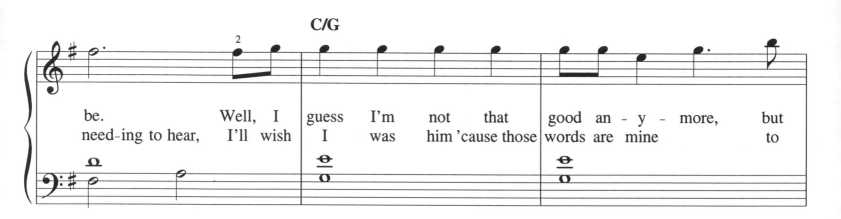

be. | Well, I | guess I'm not that | good an - y - more, but
need-ing to hear, I'll wish | I was | him 'cause those | words are mine to

ba - by that's just | me. | Yeah, I | | will
say to you 'til the | end of time. | | I | |

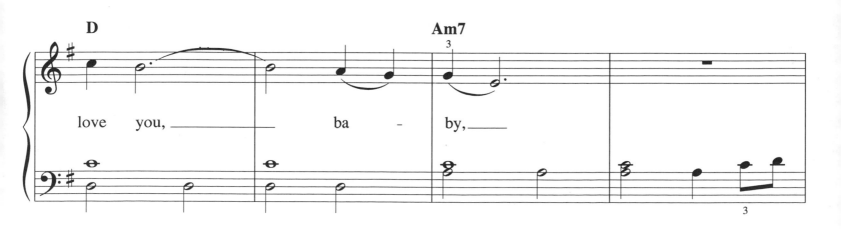

love you, | ba - by,

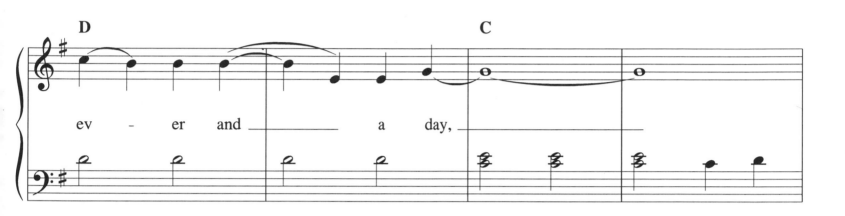

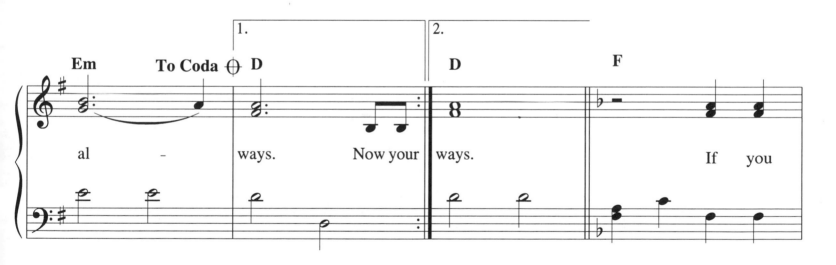

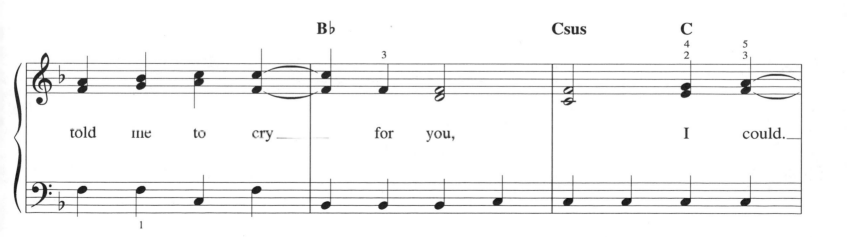

If you told me to die ___ for you ___

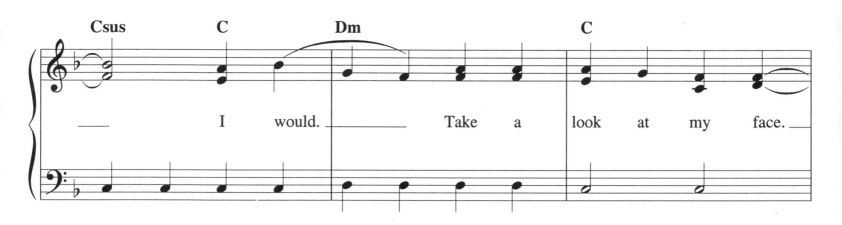

I would. ___ Take a look at my face. ___

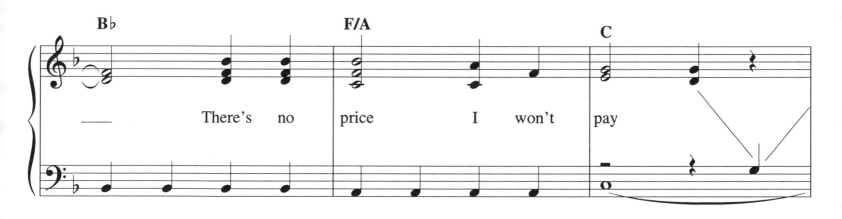

There's no price I won't pay

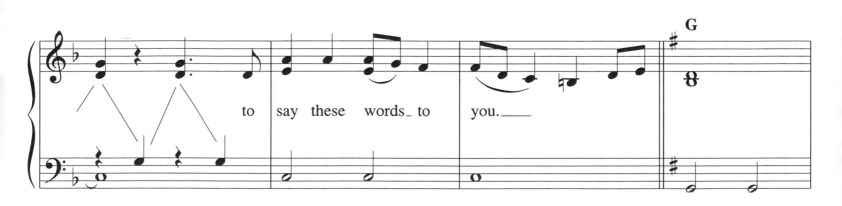

to say these words_ to you.___

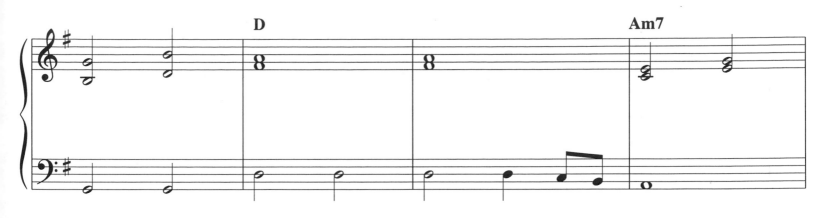

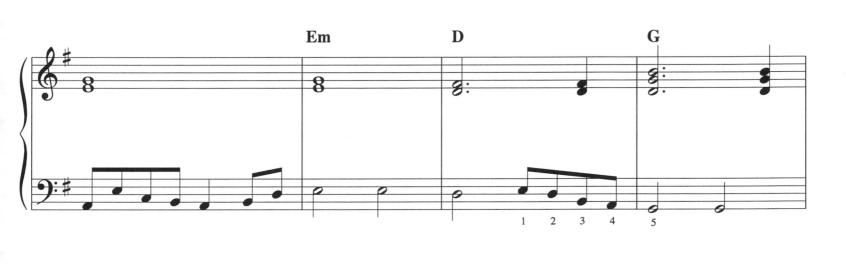

Well, there

ain't no luck in these load-ed dice, but ba-by, if you'd give me just

one more try we can pack up our old dreams and our old lives. We'll

find a place ___ where the sun still shines yeah. ___

D.S. al Coda

CODA

ways. I'll be there 'til the stars don't shine, 'til the

heav-ens burst and the words don't rhyme. I know when I die you'll be

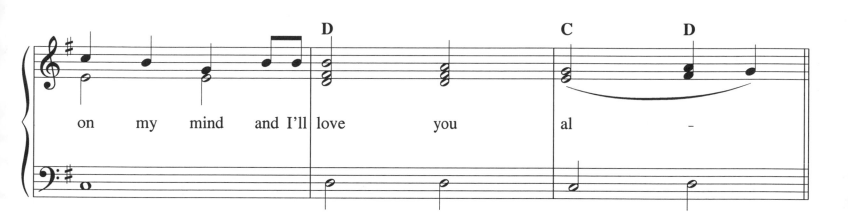

on my mind and I'll love you al -

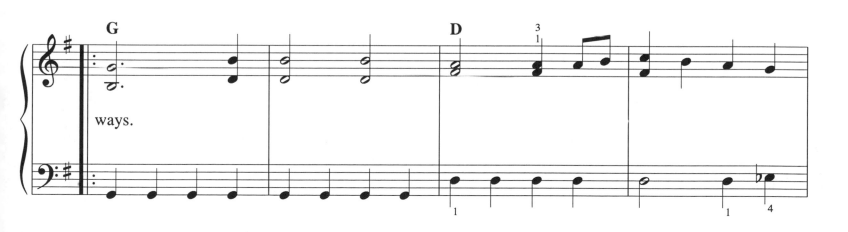

ways.

Repeat and Fade

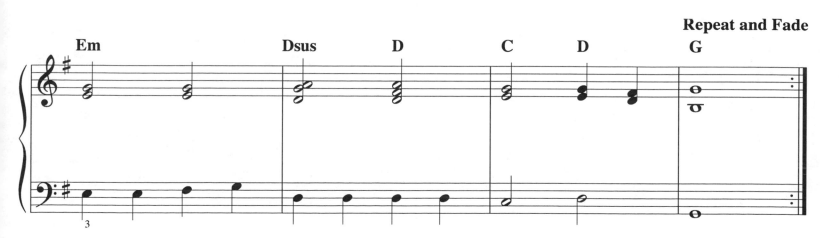

BEAUTIFUL IN MY EYES

Words and Music by
JOSHUA KADISON

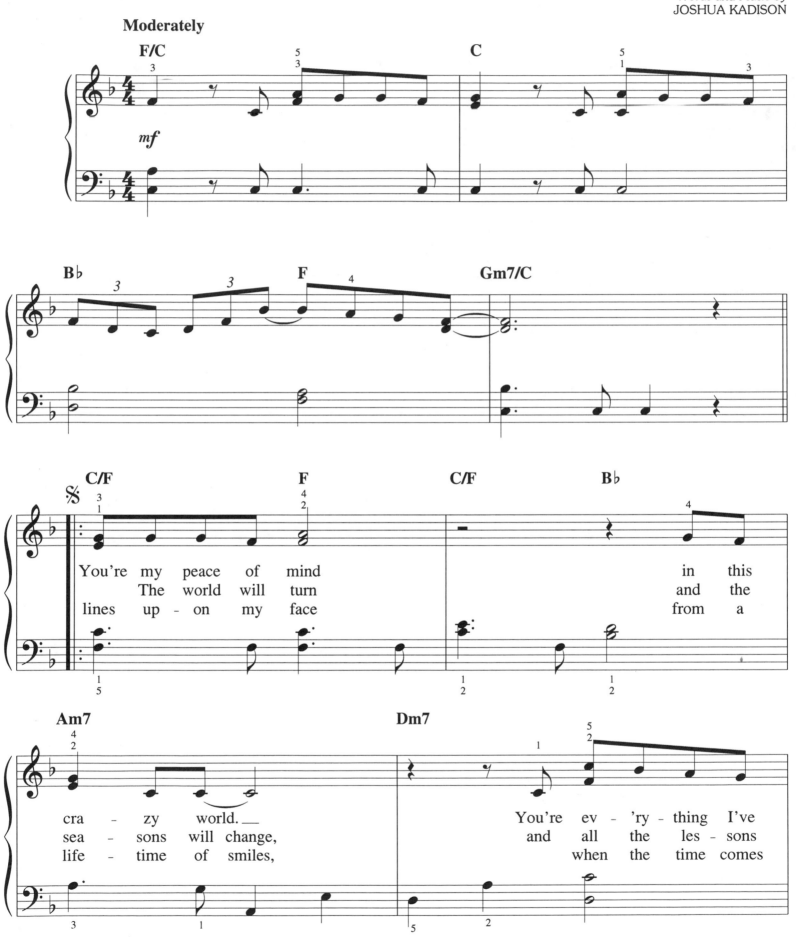

you'll al - ways be beau - ti - ful in my

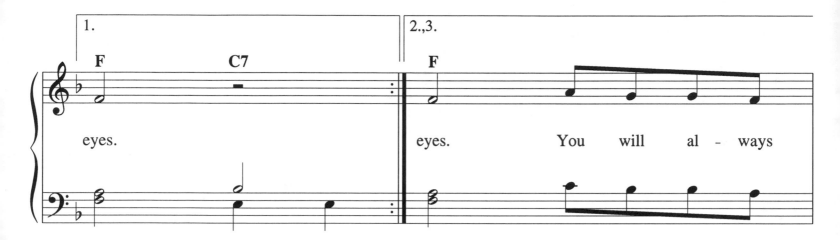

eyes. eyes. You will al - ways

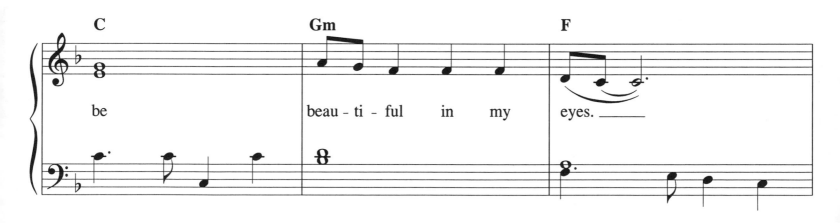

be beau - ti - ful in my eyes. _____

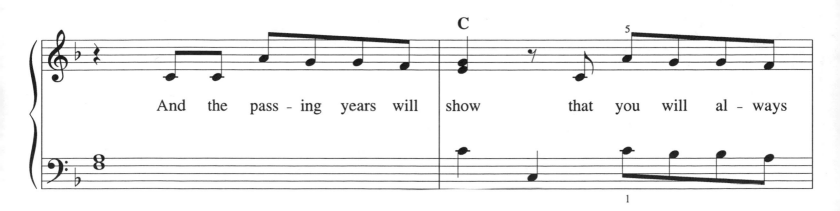

And the pass - ing years will show that you will al - ways

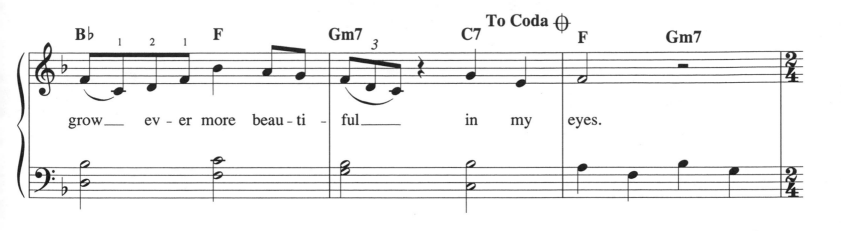

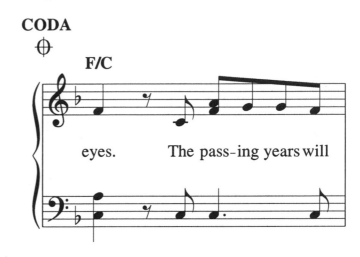

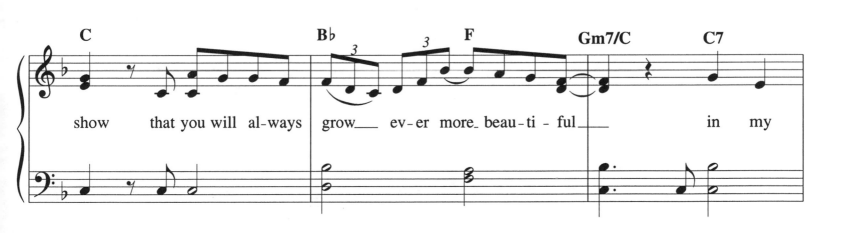

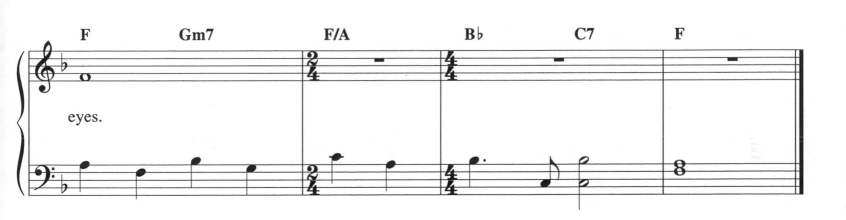

BEAUTY AND THE BEAST

from Walt Disney's BEAUTY AND THE BEAST

Lyrics by HOWARD ASHMAN
Music by ALAN MENKEN

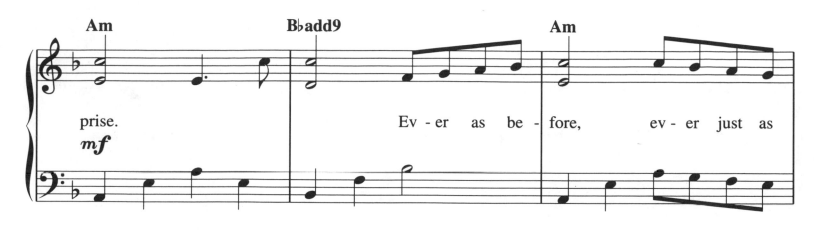

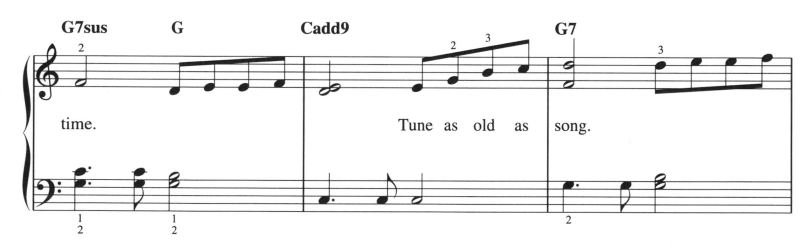

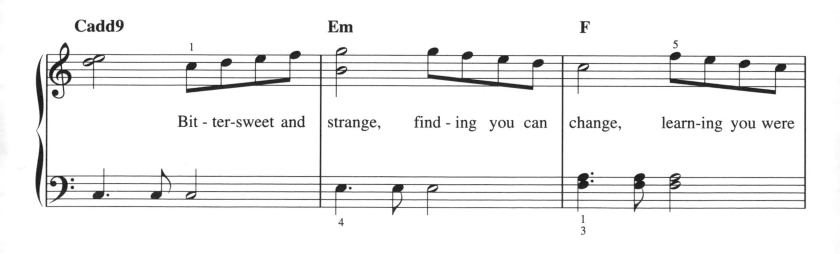

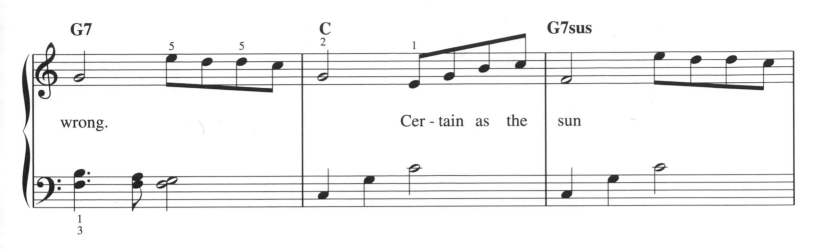

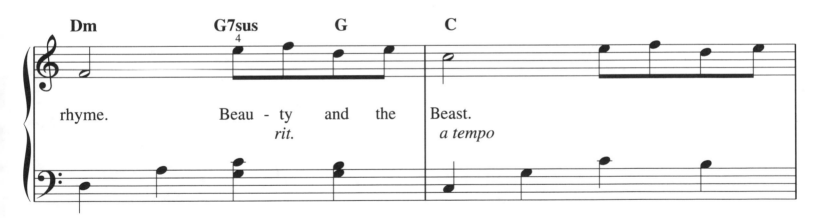

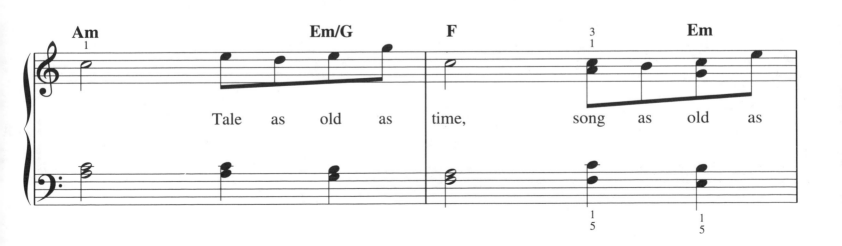

rhyme.   Beau - ty   and   the   Beast.

BLUE

Words and Music by
BILL MACK

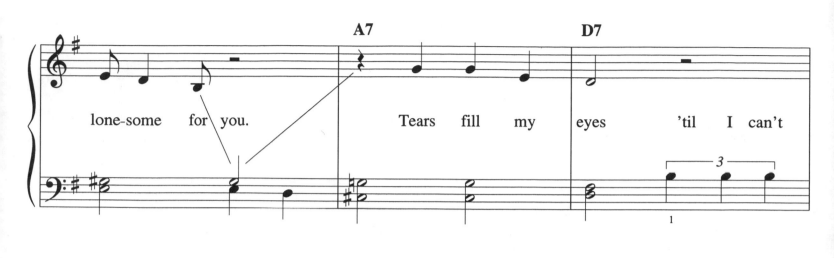

lone-some for you. Tears fill my eyes 'til I can't

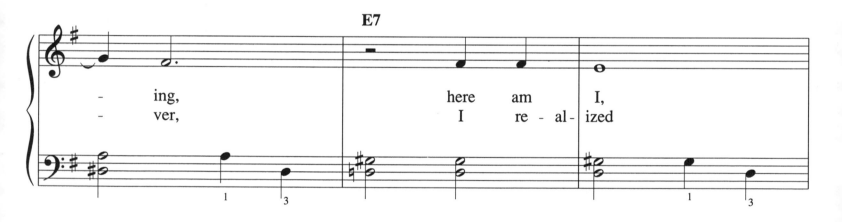

see. *Solo ends* Three o' clock in the morn -
Now that it's o -

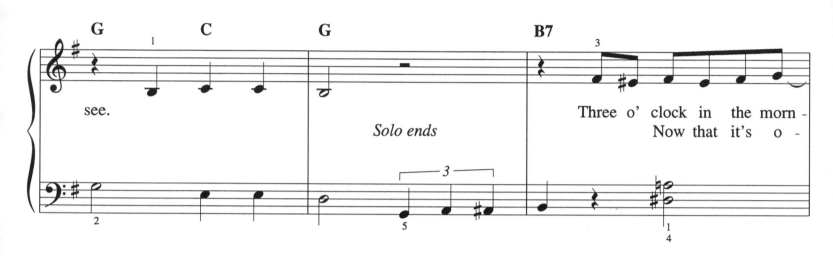

- ing, here am I,
- ver, I re - al - ized

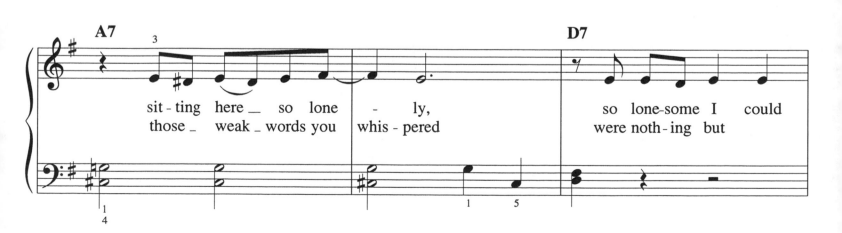

sit - ting here _ so lone - ly,
those _ weak _ words you whis - pered

so lone-some I could
were noth - ing but

BUTTERFLY KISSES

Words and Music by RANDY THOMAS
and BOB CARLISLE

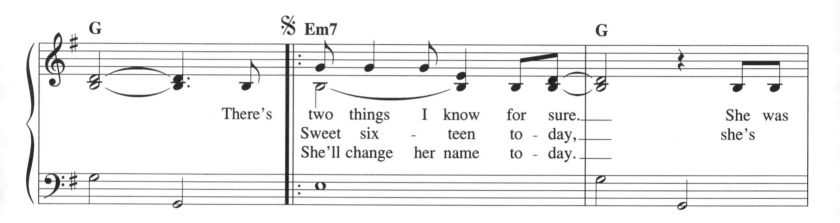

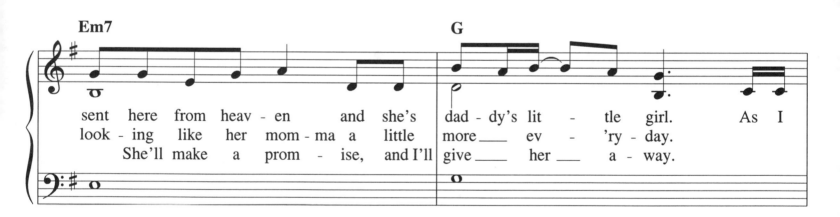

I close my eyes, and I thank God _ for all of the
rib - bons and curls try - ing _ her wings out in a
said, "I'm not sure, I just feel like _ I'm los - ing my

joy in my life. Oh, but most of all, for
great big world. _ But I re - mem - ber
ba - by girl." _ Then she leaned o - ver, gave me

but - ter - fly kiss - es ___ af - ter bed - time prayer, _ stick - in'
but - ter - fly kiss - es ___ af - ter bed - time prayer, _ stick - in'
but - ter - fly kiss - es ___ with her ma - ma there, ___ stick - in'

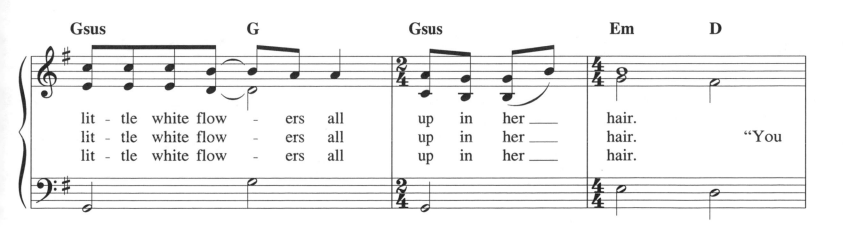

lit - tle white flow - ers all up in her ___ hair.
lit - tle white flow - ers all up in her ___ hair. "You
lit - tle white flow - ers all up in her ___ hair.

"Walk be-side __ the po - ny, dad-dy, it's my first ride. __ I
know how much __ I love you, dad-dy, but if you don't mind, __ I'm
Walk me down __ the aisle, __ dad-dy, it's just a - bout time. Does my

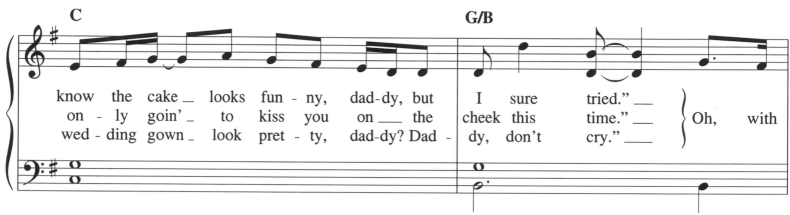

know the cake __ looks fun - ny, dad-dy, but I sure tried." __
on - ly goin' __ to kiss you on __ the cheek this time." __ } Oh, with
wed - ding gown __ look pret - ty, dad-dy? Dad - dy, don't cry." __

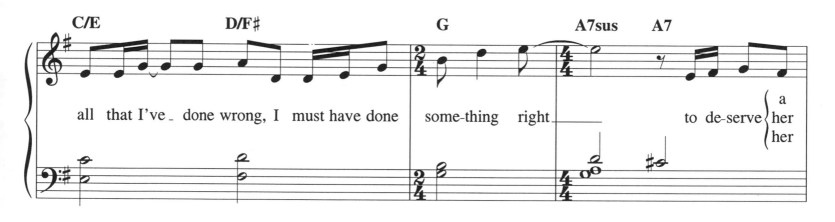

all that I've __ done wrong, I must have done some-thing right __ to de-serve { a her } { her }

To Coda ⊕

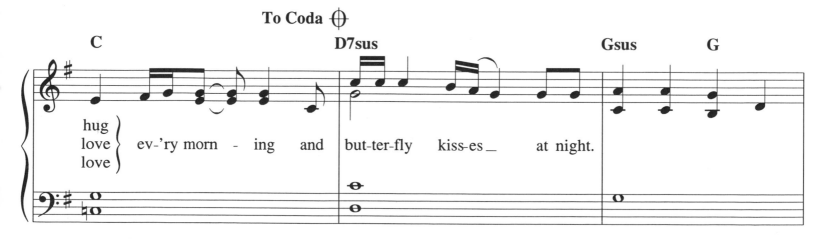

hug }
love } ev-'ry morn - ing and but-ter-fly kiss-es __ at night.
love }

CODA

but-ter-fly kiss - es. I could-n't ask God_ for more.__ Man,

this is what love _ is. I know I've got to let her go, but I'll al - ways_ re-mem-ber__ ev-'ry

molto rit. *a tempo*

hug in the morn - ing and but-ter-fly kiss-es.__

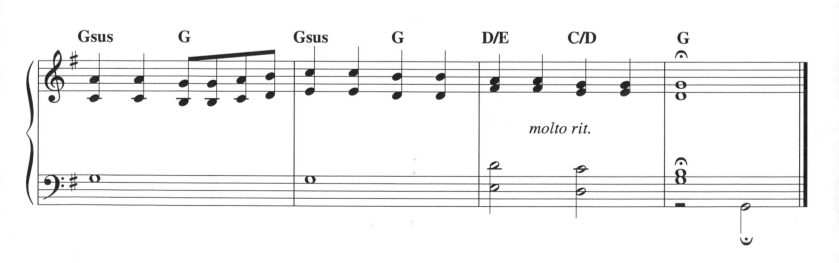

molto rit.

COLORS OF THE WIND

from Walt Disney's POCAHONTAS

Music by ALAN MENKEN
Lyrics by STEPHEN SCHWARTZ

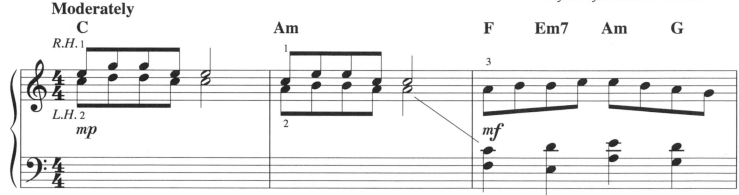

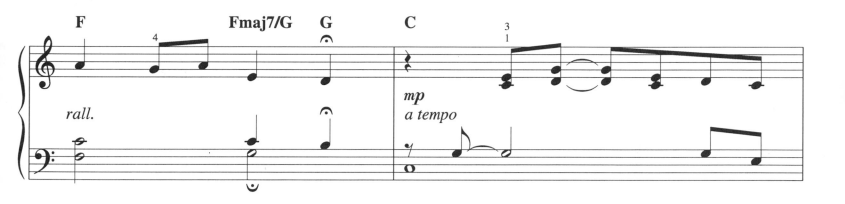

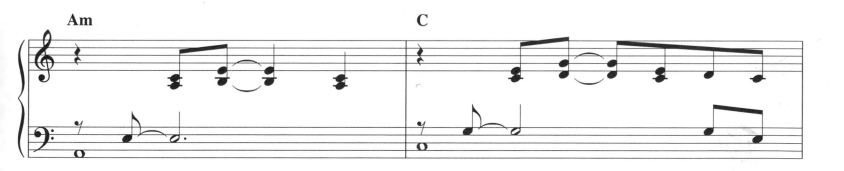

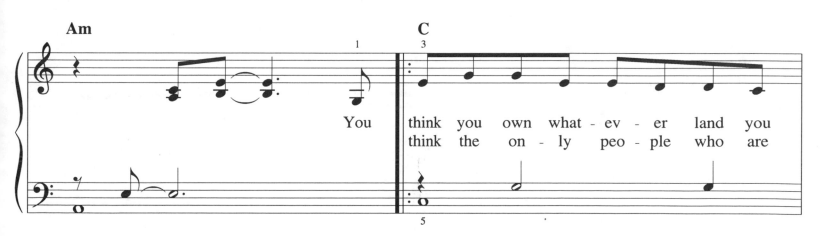

You think you own what-ev-er land you
think the on-ly peo-ple who are

Am ... **C**

land on; _____ the earth is just a dead thing you can
peo - ple are the peo - ple who look and think like

Em ... **Am** ... **Em**

claim; but I know ev - 'ry rock and tree and
you, but if you walk the foot - steps of a

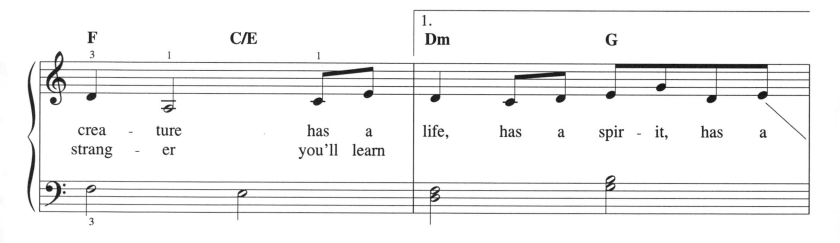

F ... **C/E** ... **1.** **Dm** ... **G**

crea - ture has a life, has a spir - it, has a
strang - er you'll learn

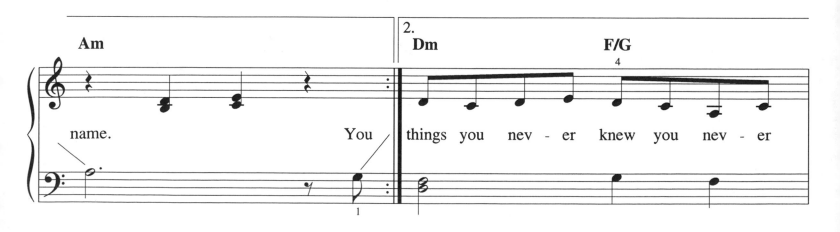

Am ... **2.** **Dm** ... **F/G**

name. You things you nev - er knew you nev - er

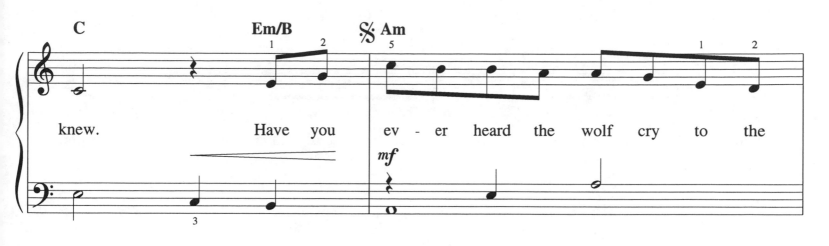

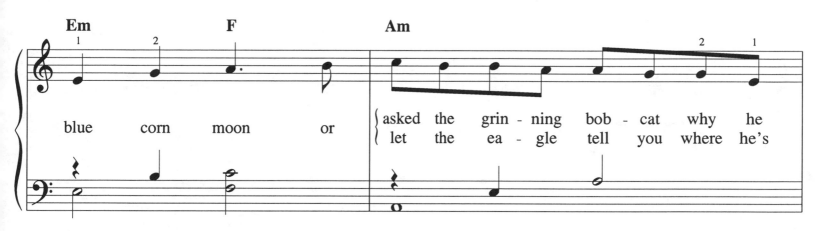

34

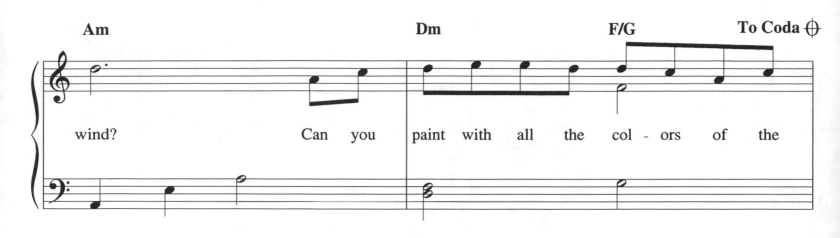

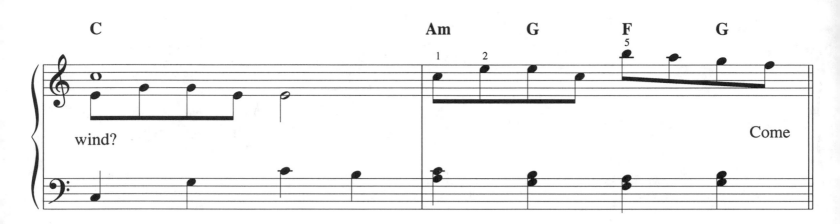

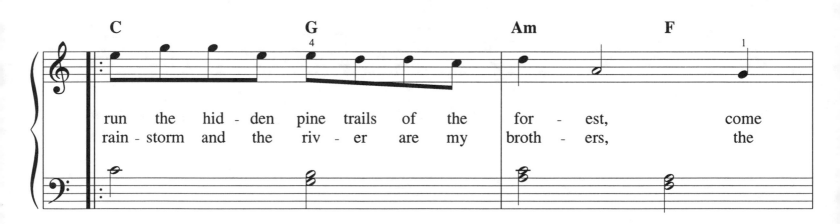

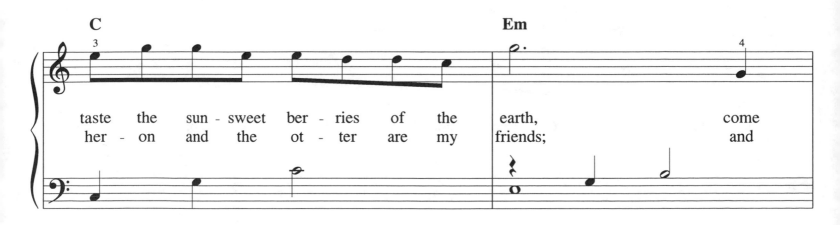

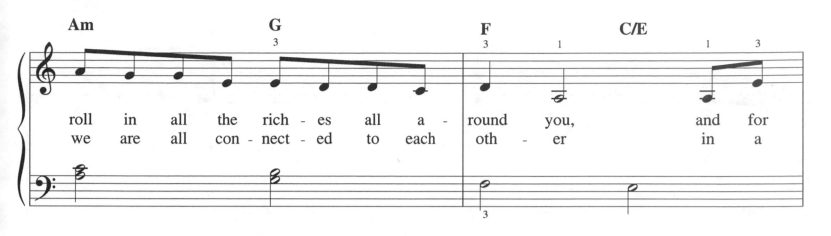

roll in all the rich - es all a - round you, and for
we are all con - nect - ed to each oth - er in a

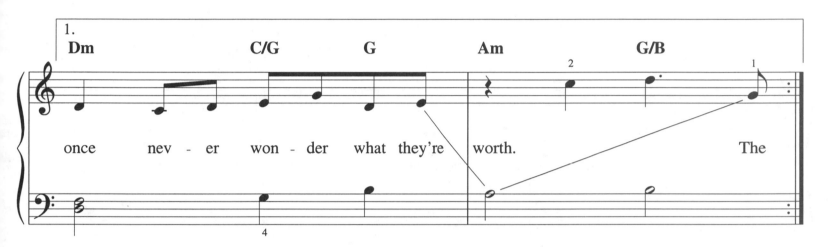

1.
once nev - er won - der what they're worth. The

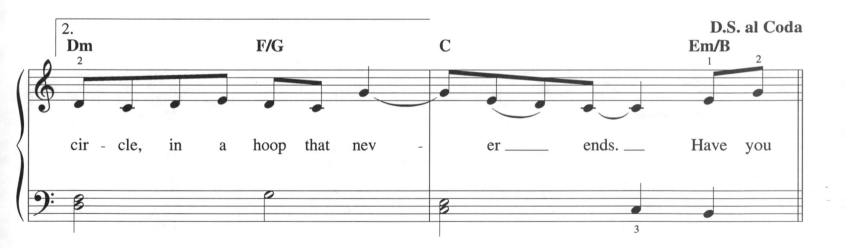

2. D.S. al Coda
cir - cle, in a hoop that nev - er ____ ends. ___ Have you

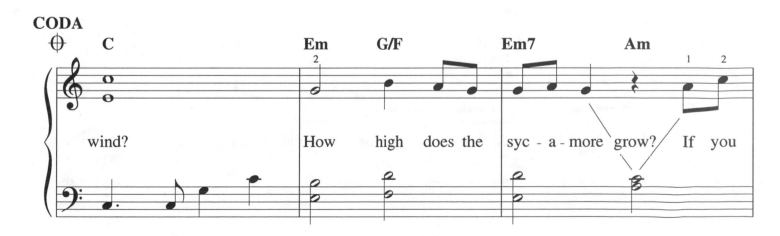

CODA
wind? How high does the syc - a - more grow? If you

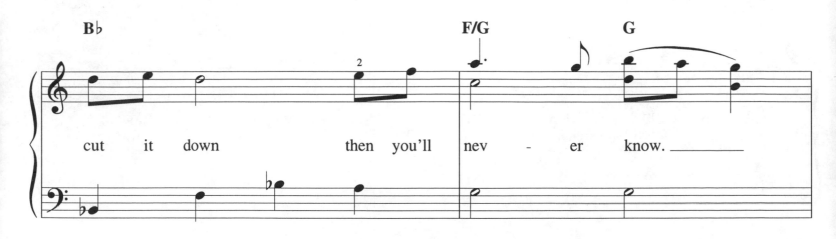

cut it down   then you'll   nev - er know. ___

And you'll nev-er hear the wolf cry to the   blue corn moon,   for

rall.   *a tempo*

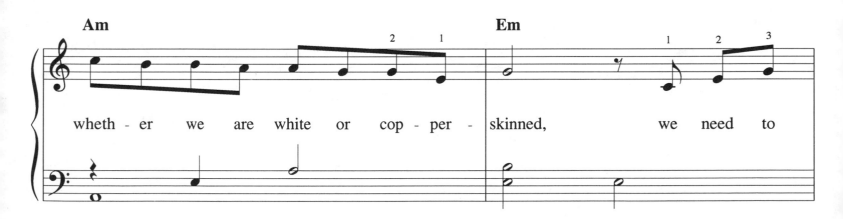

wheth - er   we   are   white   or   cop - per - skinned,   we   need   to

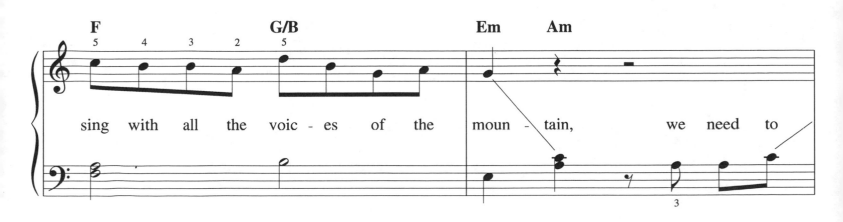

sing   with   all   the   voic - es   of   the   moun - tain,   we   need   to

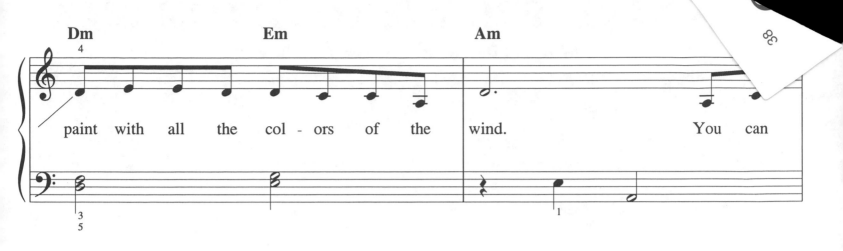

paint with all the col - ors of the wind. You can

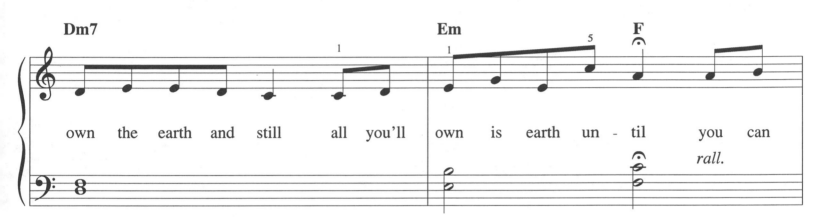

own the earth and still all you'll own is earth un - til you can
rall.

paint with all the col - ors of the wind.
a tempo

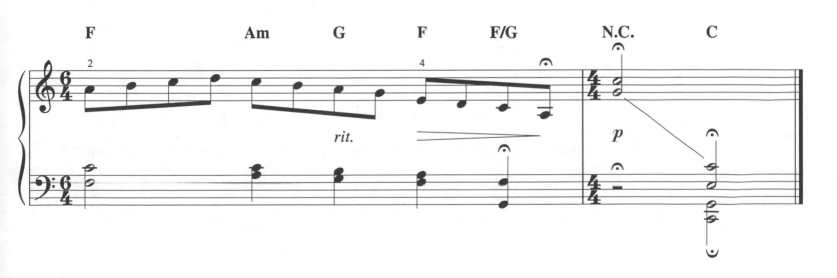

rit.

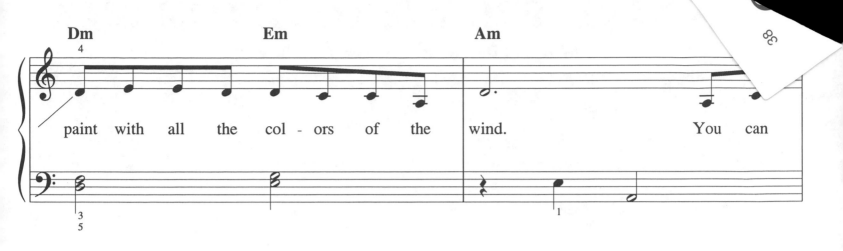

CAN YOU FEEL THE LOVE TONIGHT

from Walt Disney Pictures' THE LION KING

Music by ELTON JOHN
Lyrics by TIM RICE

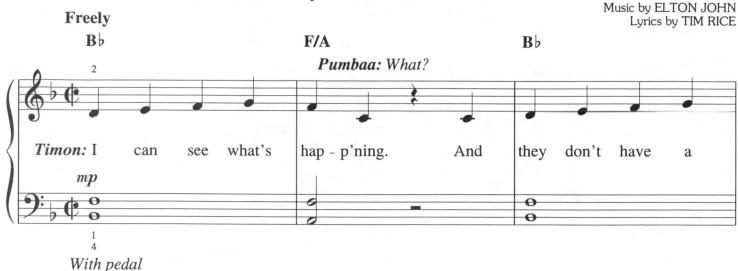

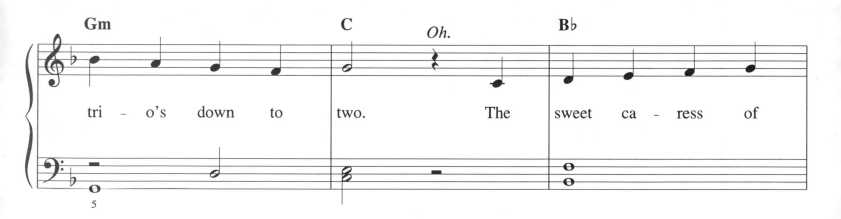

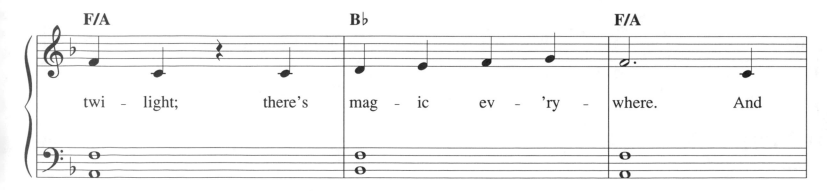

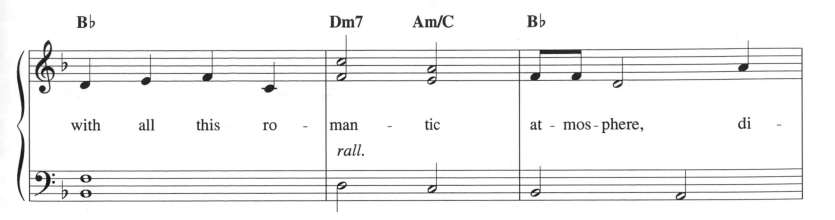

with all this ro - man - tic at - mos - phere, di -
rall.

Moderately (in two)

sas - ter's in the air. cresc.
a tempo

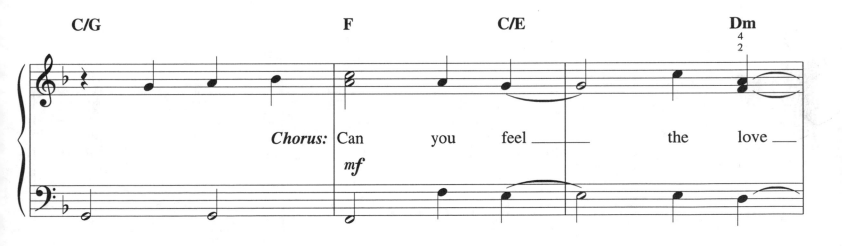

Chorus: Can you feel the love
mf

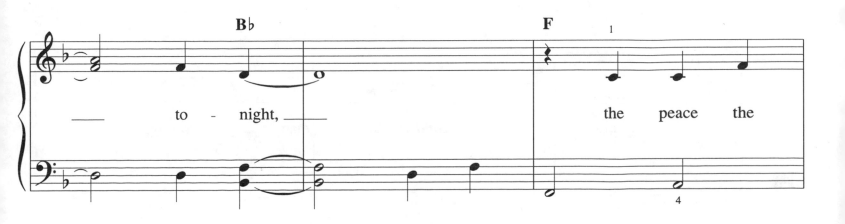

to - night, the peace the

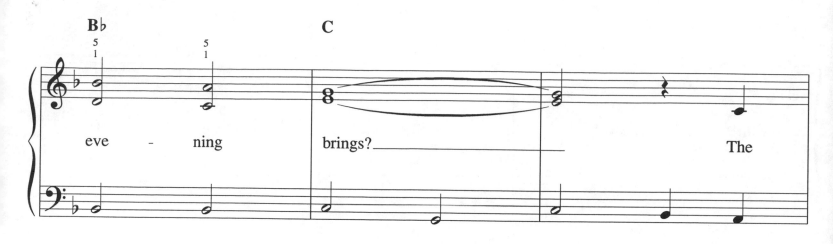

eve - ning brings?_____ The

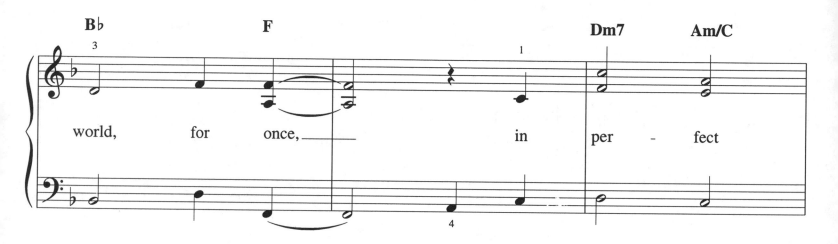

world, for once,_____ in per - fect

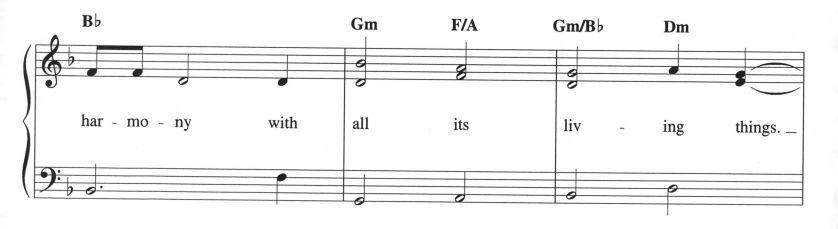

har - mo - ny with all its liv - ing things.__

dim.

Simba: So man - y things to
mp

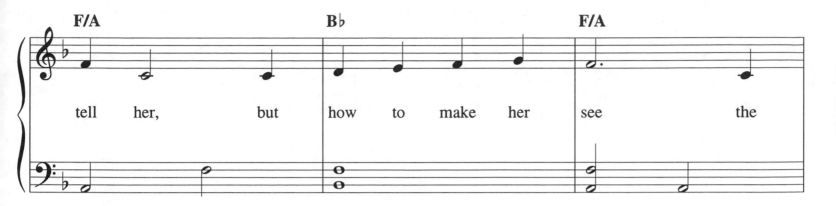

F/A — **B♭** — **F/A**

tell her, but how to make her see the

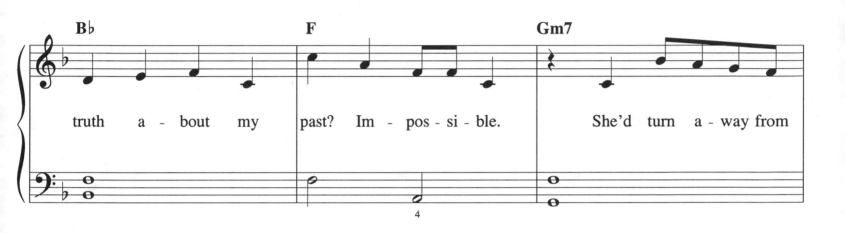

B♭ — **F** — **Gm7**

truth a - bout my past? Im - pos - si - ble. She'd turn a - way from

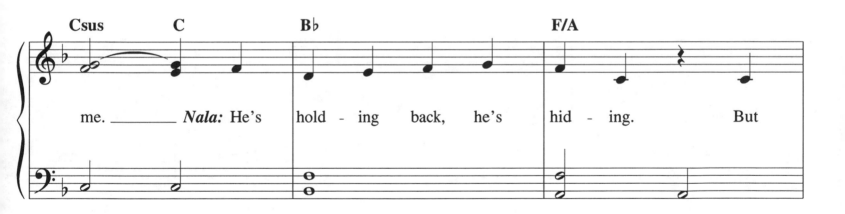

Csus **C** — **B♭** — **F/A**

me. _____ *Nala:* He's hold - ing back, he's hid - ing. But

B♭ — **F/A** — **B♭**

what? I can't de - cide. Why won't he be the

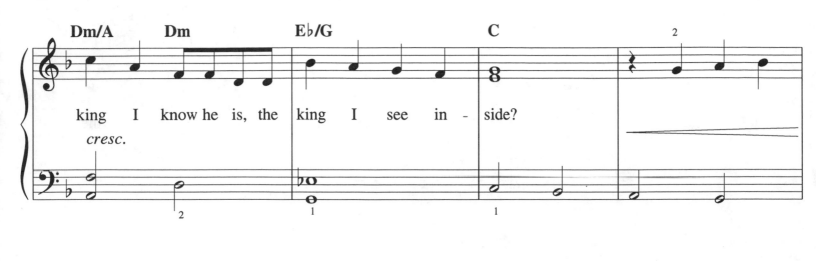

king I know he is, the king I see in - side?

Chorus:
Can you feel ____ the love ____ to - night, ____

____ the peace the eve - ning brings? ____

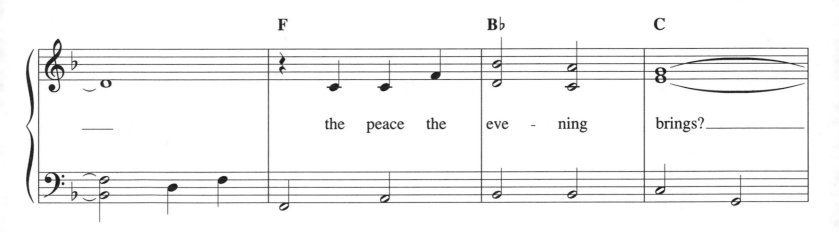

____ The world, for once, ____ in

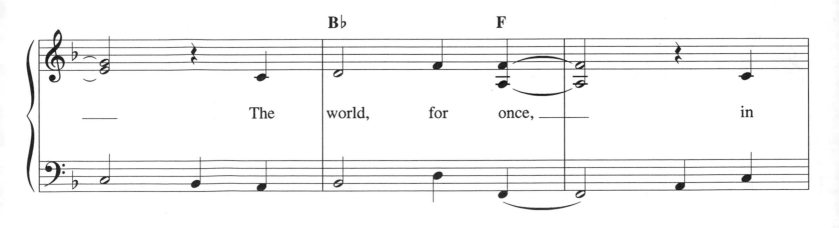

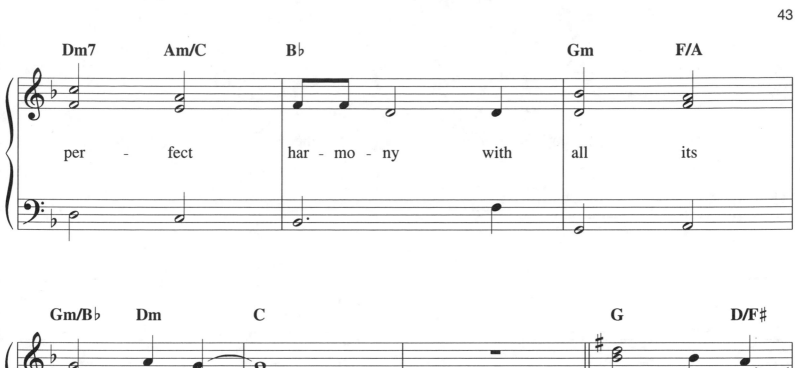

per - fect   har - mo - ny   with   all   its

liv - ing   things.   _____   Can   you   feel _____

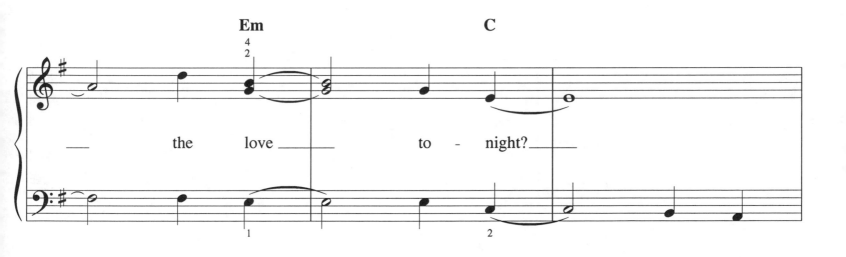

_____ the   love _____   to - night? _____

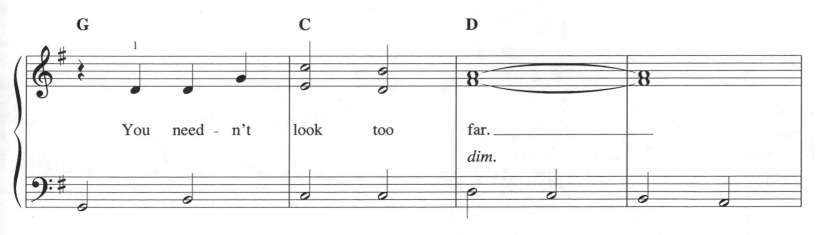

You   need - n't   look   too   far. _____

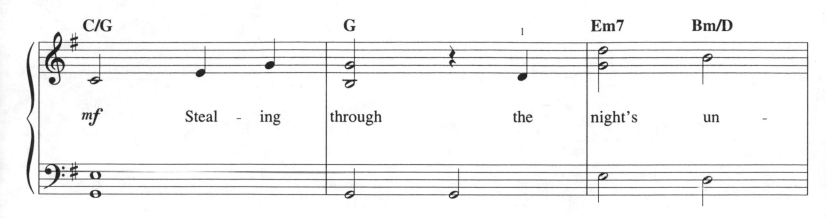

Steal - ing   through   the   night's   un -

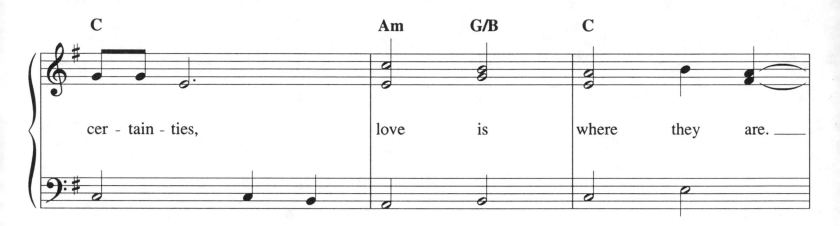

cer - tain - ties,   love   is   where   they   are.___

___   *Timon:* And   if   he

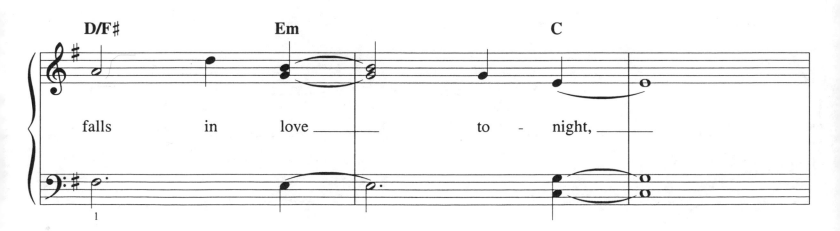

falls   in   love ___   to - night, ___

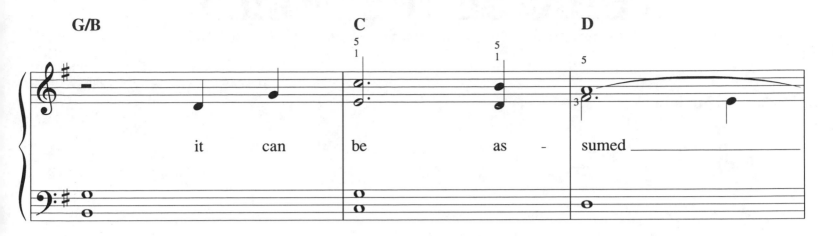

it can be as - sumed _____

_____ *Pumbaa:* his care - free days with

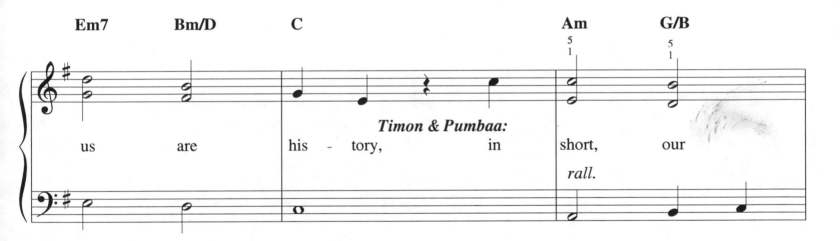

us are his - tory, in short, our

Timon & Pumbaa:

rall.

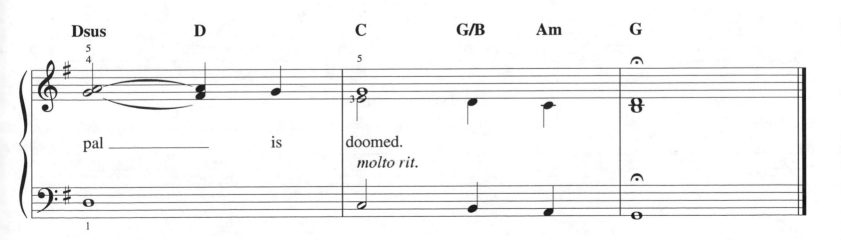

pal _____ is doomed.

molto rit.

CHANGE THE WORLD

featured on the Motion Picture Soundtrack PHENOMENON

Words and Music by GORDON KENNEDY,
TOMMY SIMS and WAYNE KIRKPATRICK

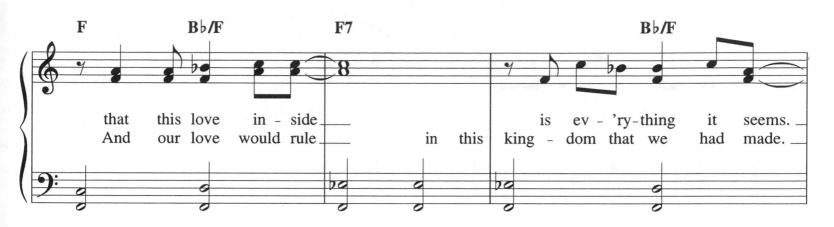

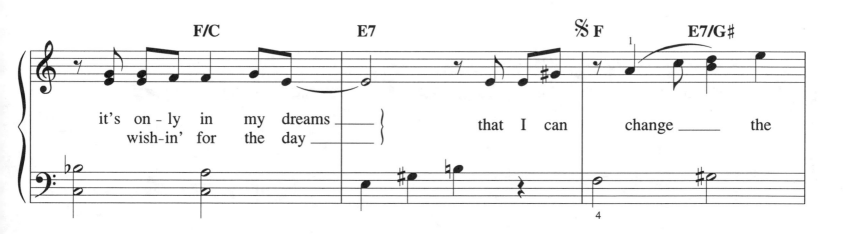

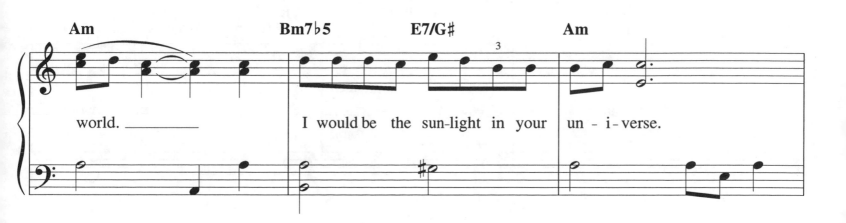

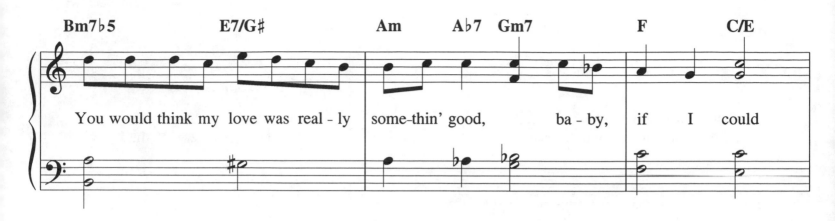

You would think my love was real-ly some-thin' good, ba-by, if I could

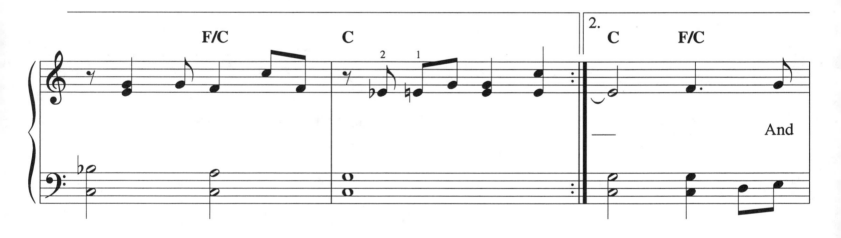

change _____ the world. ____

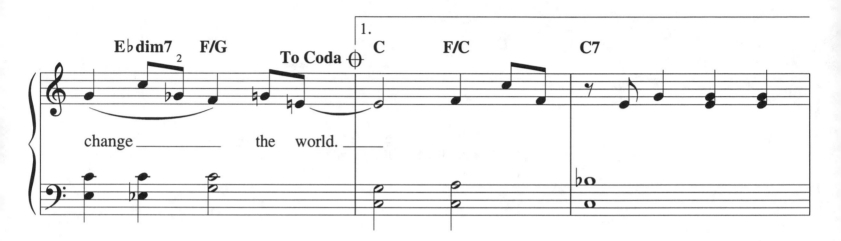

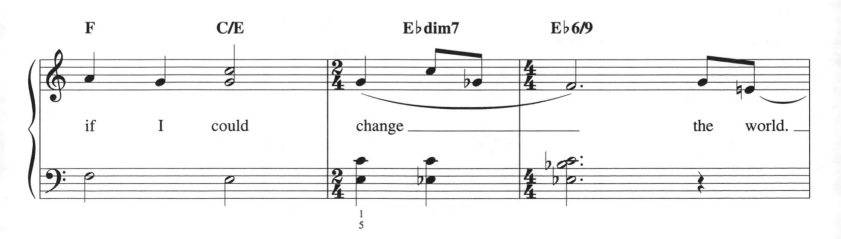

if I could change _____ the world. ___

And

DON'T CRY FOR ME ARGENTINA
from EVITA

Words by TIM RICE
Music by ANDREW LLOYD WEBBER

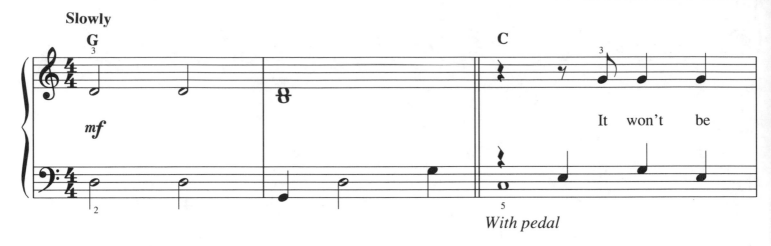

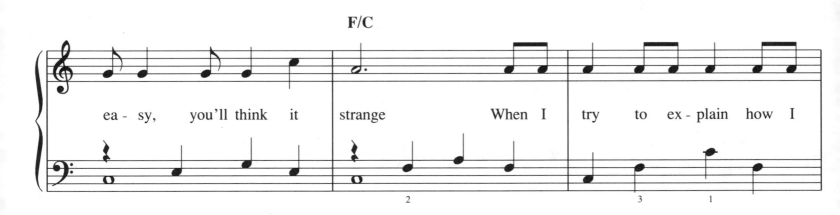

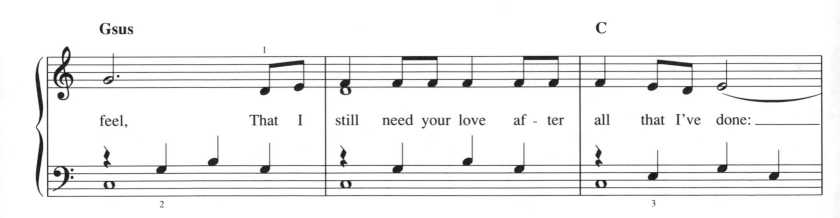

MCA Music Publishing

Am/C

You won't be - lieve me   All you will see is a

D   **D7/C**   **G/B**

girl you once knew   Al - though she's dressed up to the nines   at

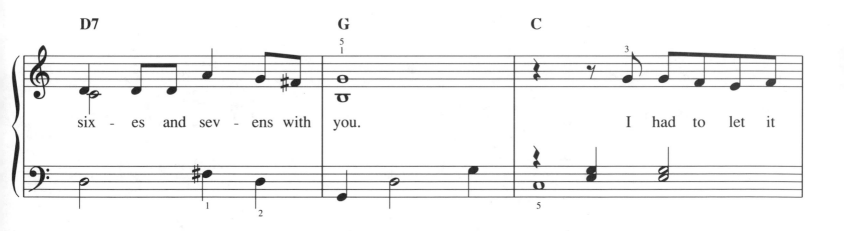

D7   **G**   **C**

six - es and sev - ens with you.   I had to let it

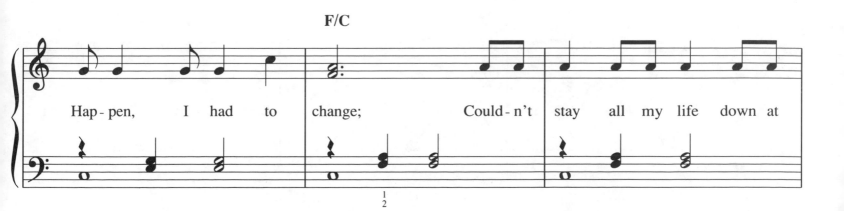

F/C

Hap - pen, I had to change;   Could - n't stay all my life down at

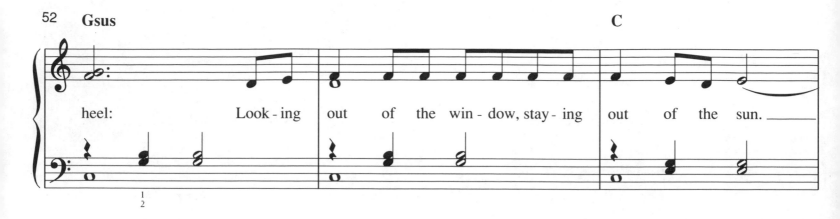

heel: Look - ing out of the win - dow, stay - ing out of the sun.

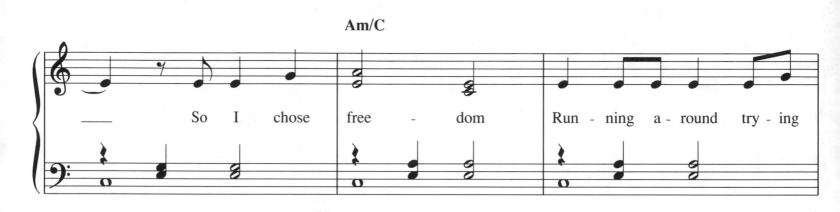

So I chose free - dom Run - ning a - round try - ing

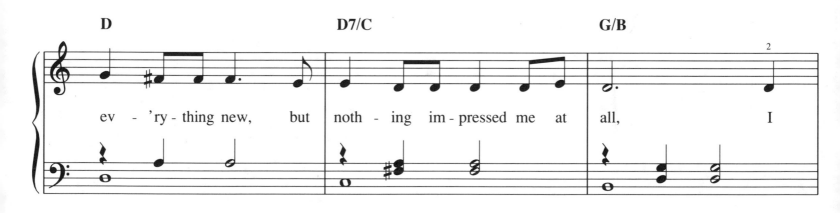

ev - 'ry - thing new, but noth - ing im - pressed me at all, I

nev - er ex - pect - ed it to. Don't cry for me Ar - gen -

53

ENDLESS LOVE

Words and Music by
LIONEL RICHIE

Moderately flowing

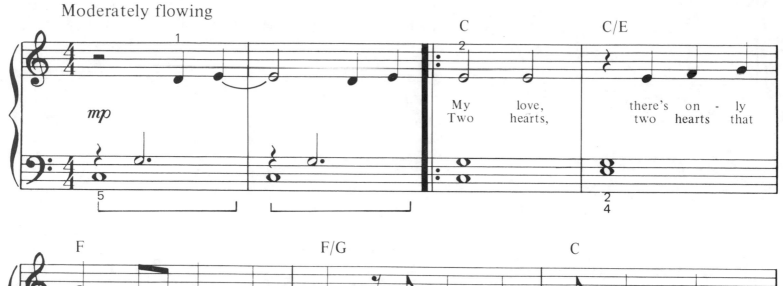

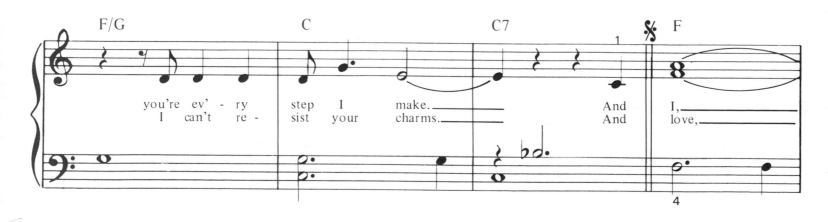

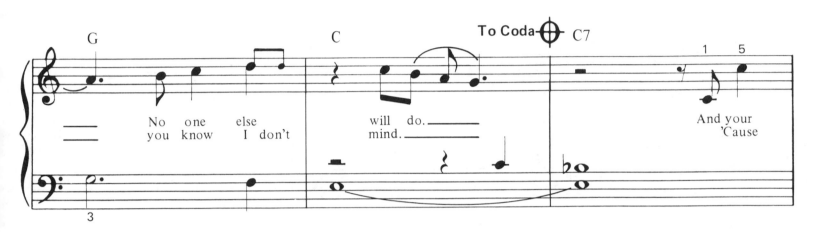

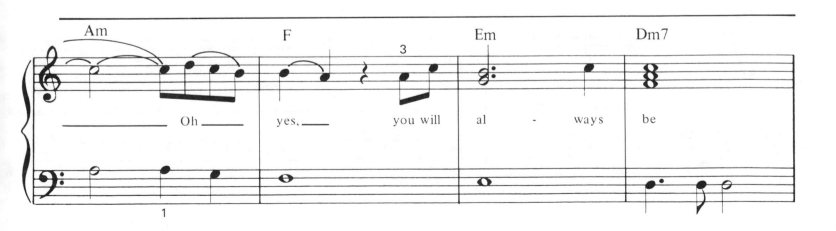

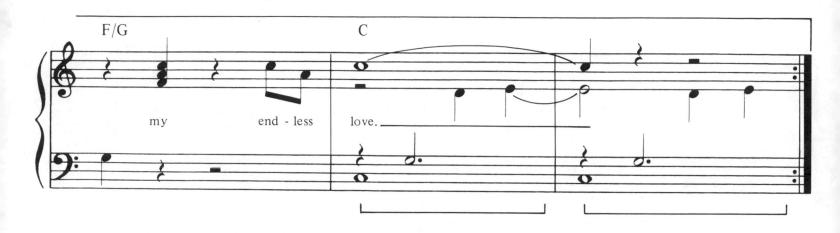

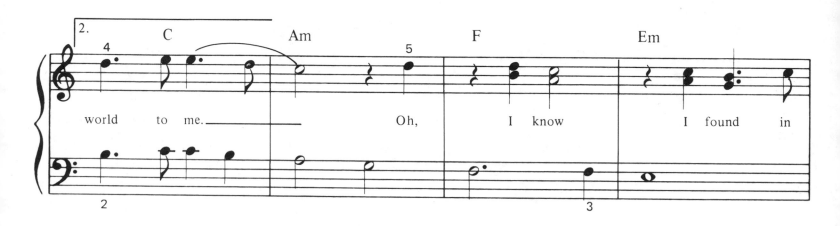

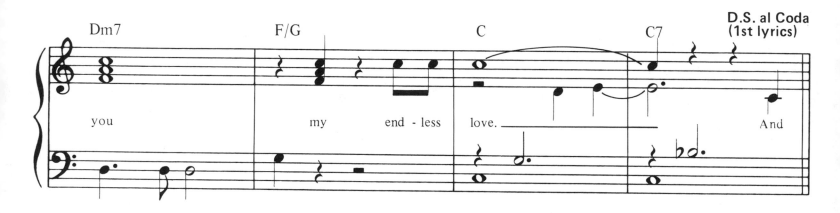

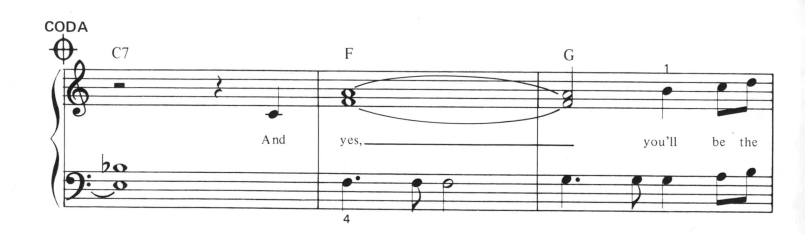

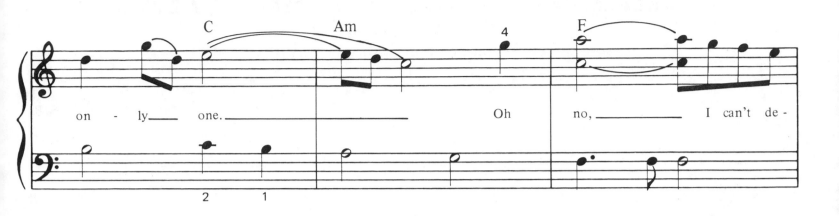

on - ly____ one. _____ Oh no, _____ I can't de -

ny this love, _____ I have in - side, and I'll

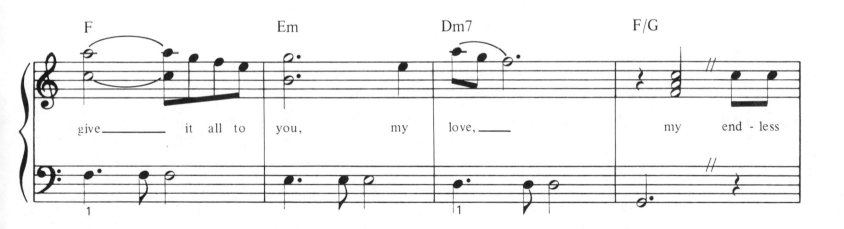

give____ it all to you, my love, ____ my end - less

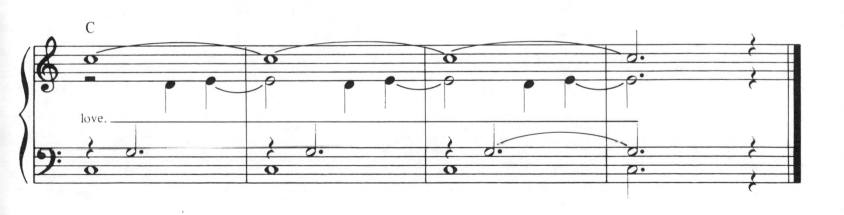

love. _____

FORREST GUMP – MAIN TITLE
(Feather Theme)
from the Paramount Motion Picture FORREST GUMP

Music by ALAN SILVESTRI

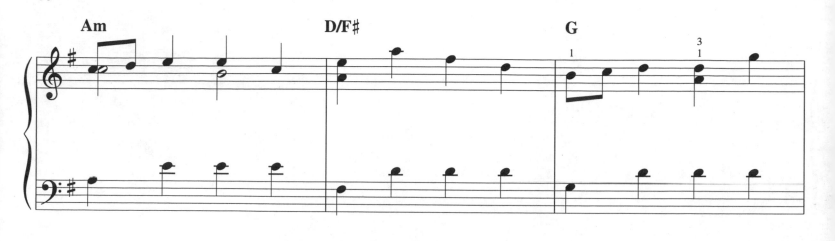

FIELDS OF GOLD

Written and Composed by
STING

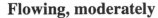

Flowing, moderately

You'll re-

mem-ber me ___ when the west wind moves ___ up-on the fields ___ of
stay with me, ___ will you be my love ___ a-mong the fields ___ of

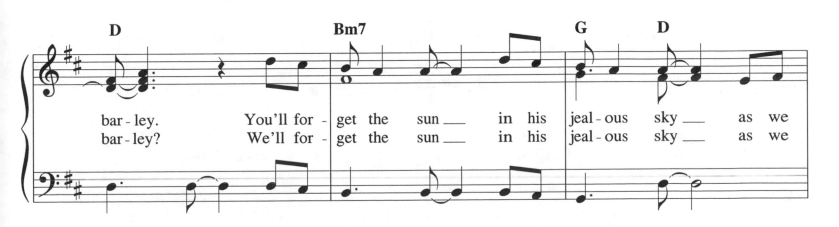

bar-ley. You'll for-get the sun ___ in his jeal-ous sky ___ as we
bar-ley? We'll for-get the sun ___ in his jeal-ous sky ___ as we

64

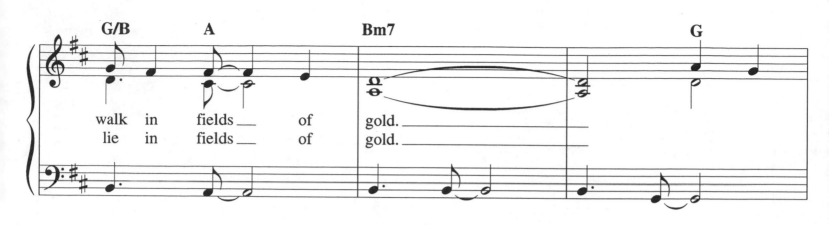

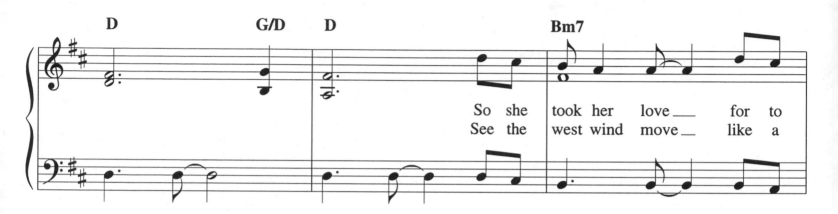

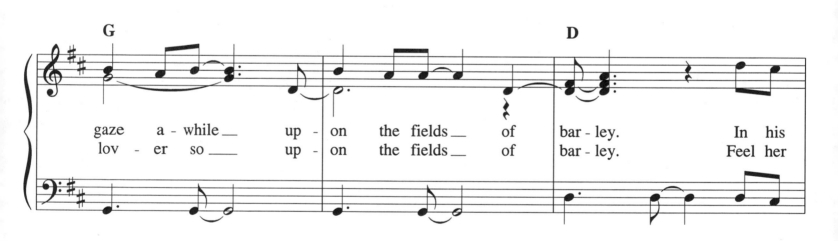

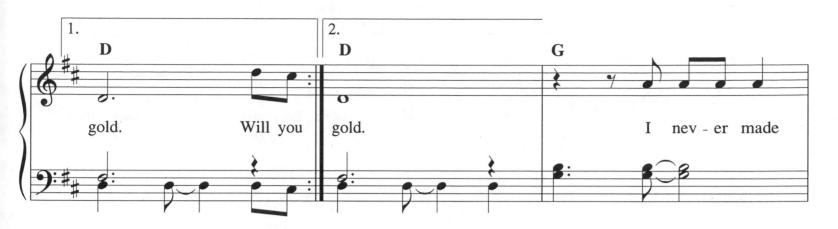

gold.　Will you　gold.　　　　　　　　　　I　nev - er made

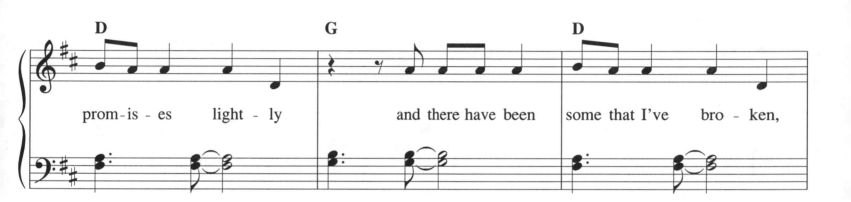

prom-is - es　light - ly　　and there have been　some that I've　bro - ken,

but I swear＿ in the　days still　left we'll　walk　in fields＿　of

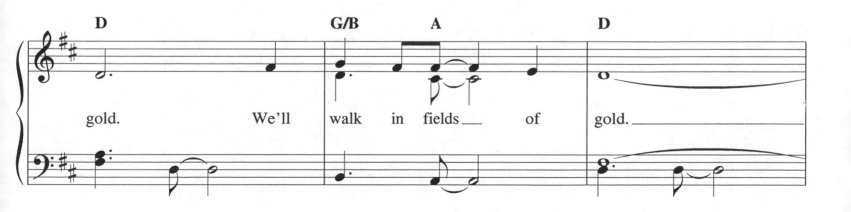

gold.　　We'll　walk　in fields＿　of　gold.＿＿＿＿＿

66

67

gold. You'll re- gold, when we walked in fields of

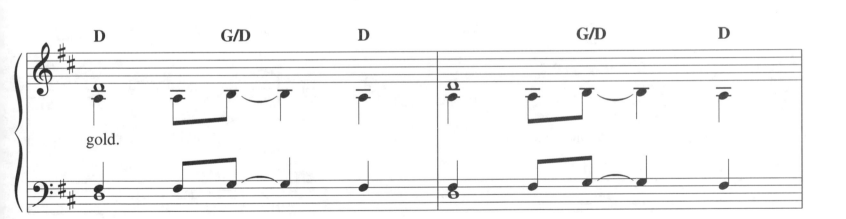

gold, when we walked in fields of

gold.

HAVE I TOLD YOU LATELY

Words and Music by
VAN MORRISON

HERO

Words and Music by MARIAH CAREY
and WALTER AFANASIEFF

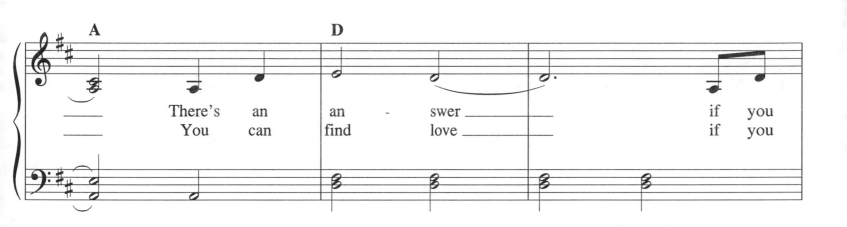

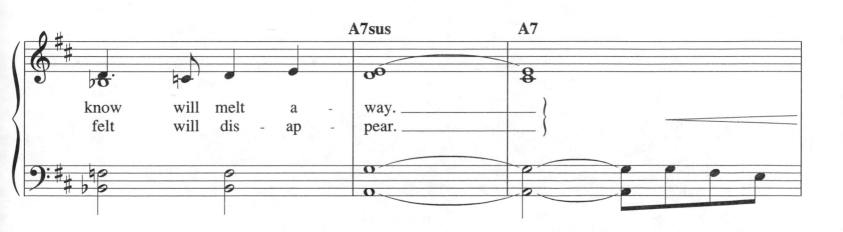

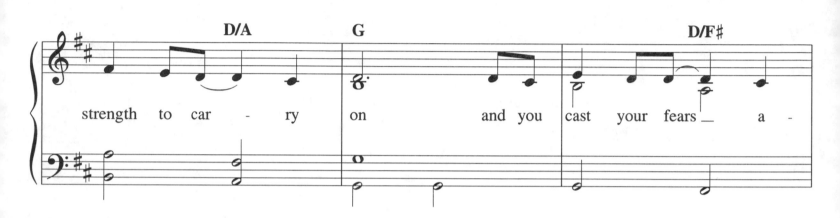

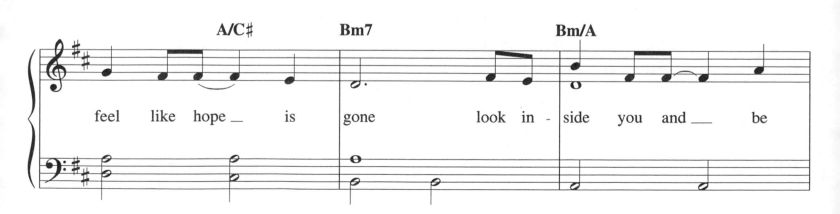

strong and you'll fi - n'lly see ___ the truth that a

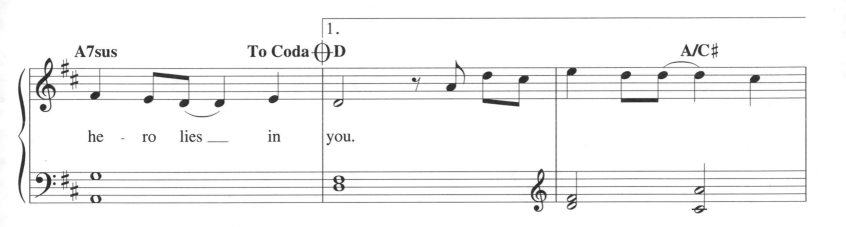

he - ro lies ___ in you.

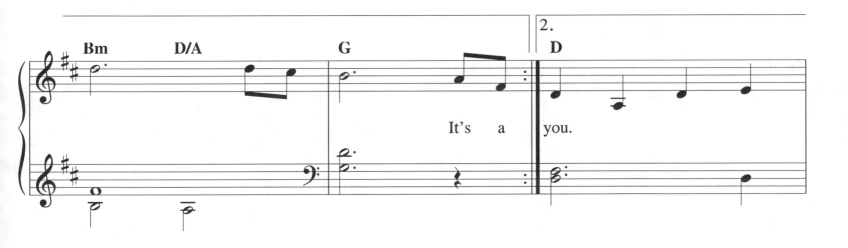

It's a you.

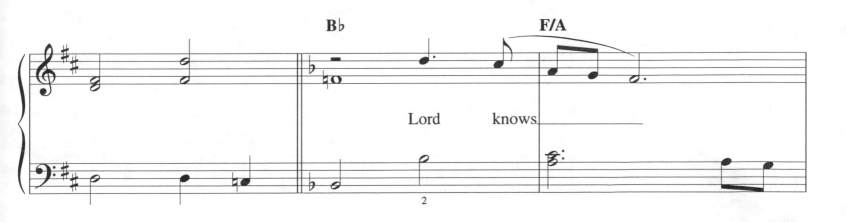

Lord knows ___

2

dreams are hard to fol - low, but don't let

an - y - one tear them a - way.

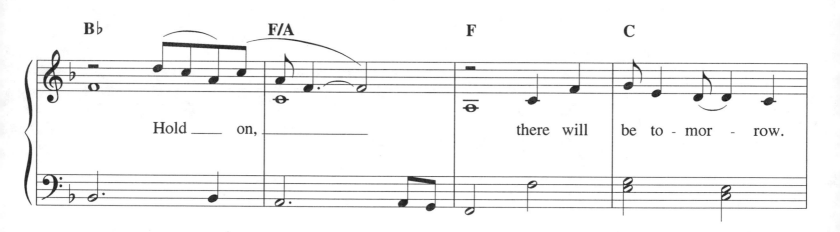

Hold ____ on, ____ there will be to-mor - row.

In ____ time ____ you'll find the way. ____ rall.

D.S. al Coda

77

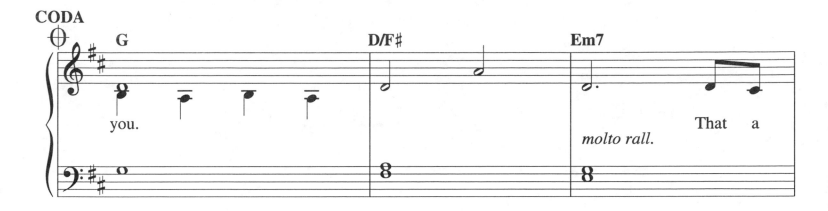

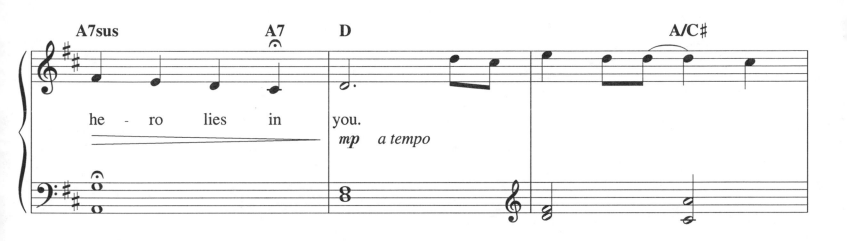

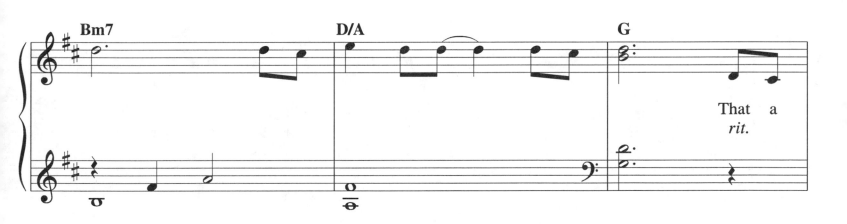

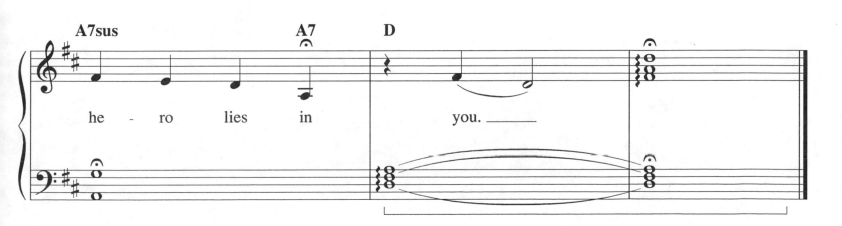

I BELIEVE IN YOU AND ME

from the Touchstone Motion Picture THE PREACHER'S WIFE

Words and Music by DAVID WOLFERT
and SANDY LINZER

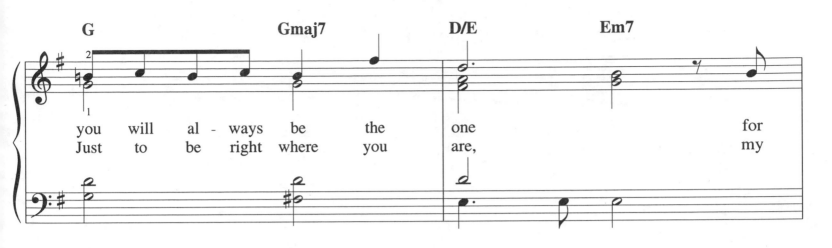

you will al - ways be the one are, for
Just to be right where you my

me. _____ Oh, yes, you will. And I be-lieve in
love. _____ You know I love you, boy. I'll nev - er

dreams a - gain. _____ I be-lieve that love will nev - er end. And
leave you out. _____ I will al - ways let you in, boy oh ba - by, to

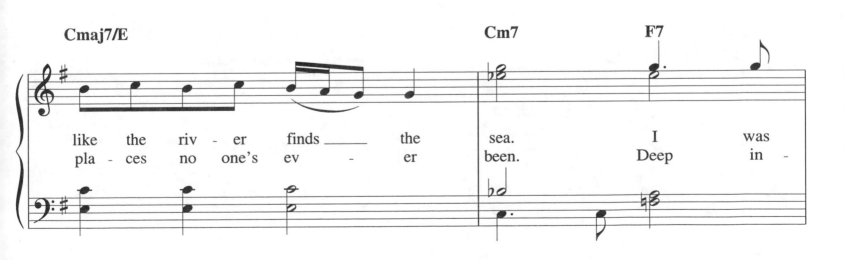

like the riv - er finds _____ the sea. I was
pla - ces no one's ev - er been. Deep in -

I be - lieve, _ I do be - lieve in you and me. _____ See, I'm ____

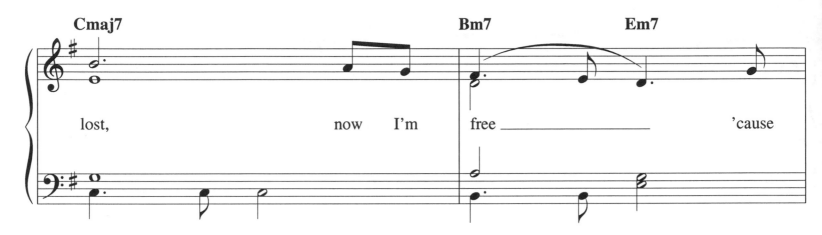

lost, now I'm free _____ 'cause

I be-lieve in you and me.

I CAN LOVE YOU LIKE THAT

Words and Music by STEVE DIAMOND,
MARIBETH DERRY and JENNIFER KIMBALL

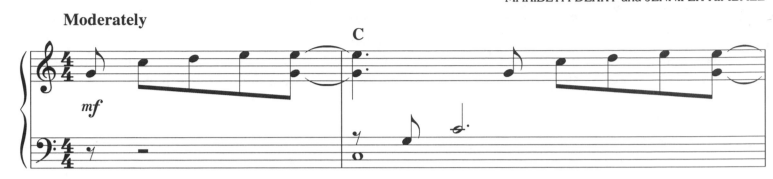

read you Cin - der - el - la   you   hoped   it   would   come true   that
nev - er   make   a   prom - ise   I   don't   in - tend   to   keep.   So,

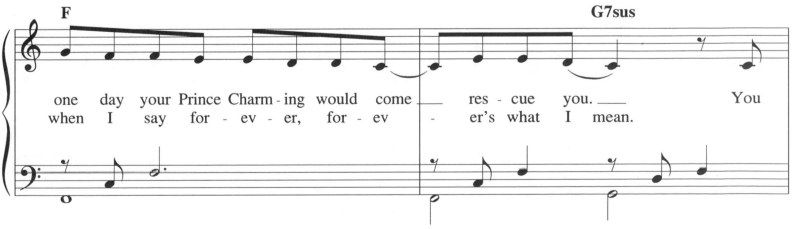

one   day   your   Prince   Charm - ing   would   come ____   res - cue   you. ____   You
when   I   say   for - ev - er,   for - ev - er's   what   I   mean.

I can love you like that. I would make you my world, move heav-en and earth

if you were my girl. I will give you my heart, be all that you need,

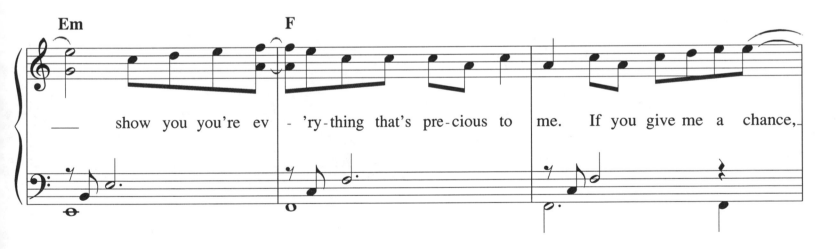

show you you're ev-'ry-thing that's pre-cious to me. If you give me a chance,

I can love you like that.

I FINALLY FOUND SOMEONE
from THE MIRROR HAS TWO FACES

Words and Music by BARBRA STREISAND, MARVIN HAMLISCH,
R.J. LANGE and BRYAN ADAMS

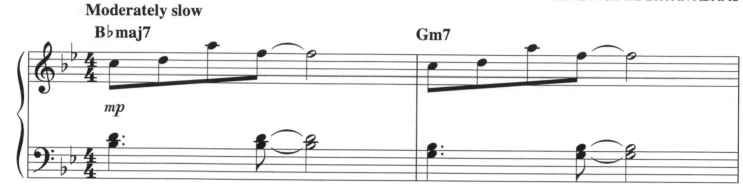

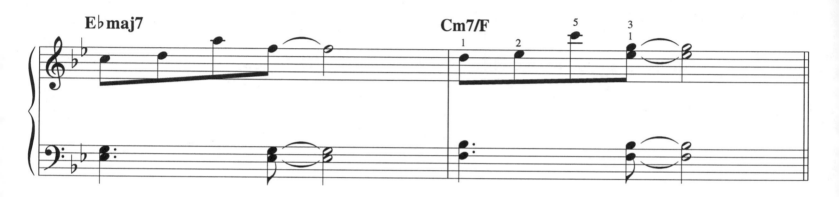

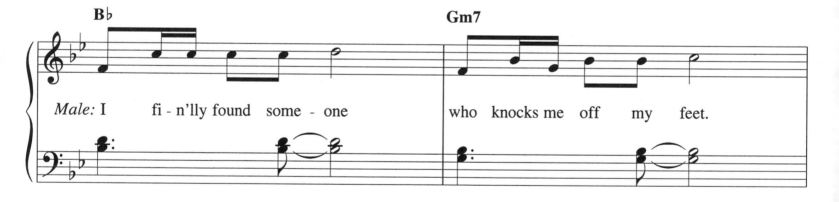

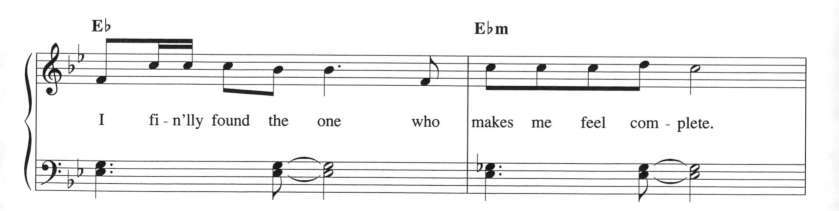

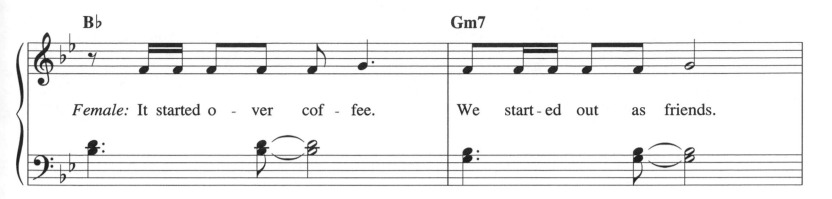

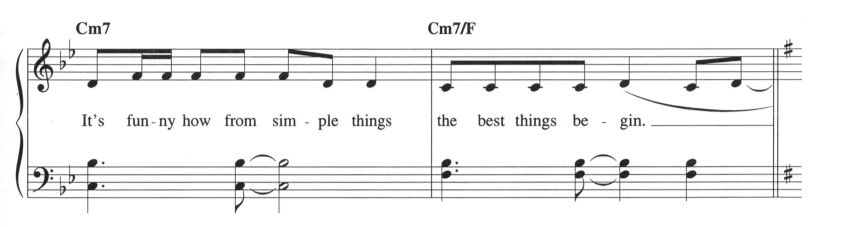

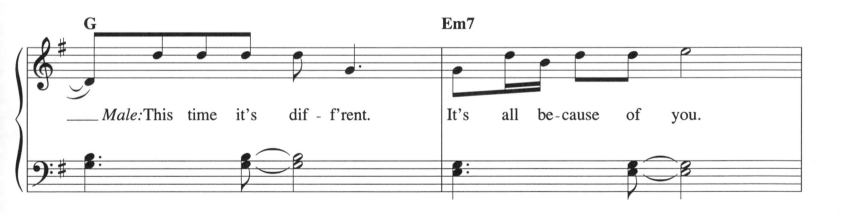

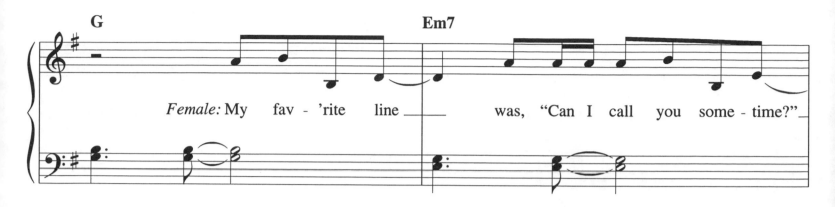

be with ev - 'ry night. *Female:* 'Cause what - ev - er I do,___ *Male:* it's just

got to be you.___ *Both:* My life has just be - gun, I fi - n'lly

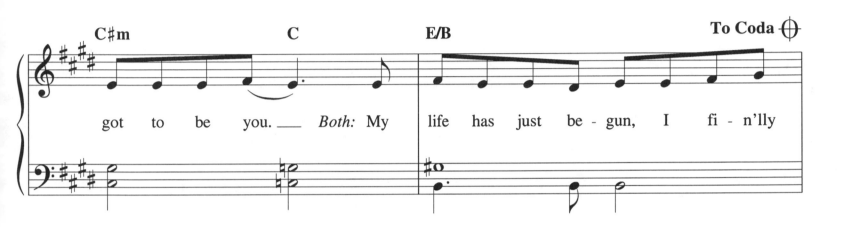

found some - one.

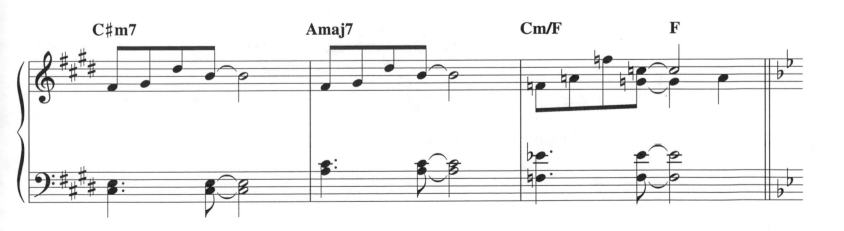

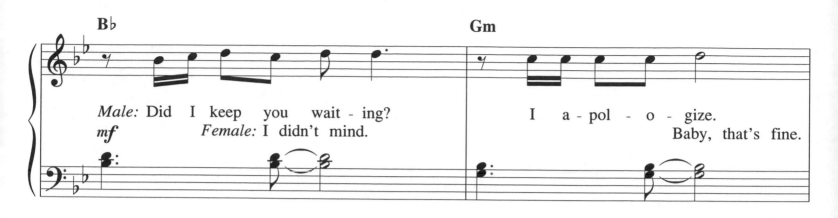

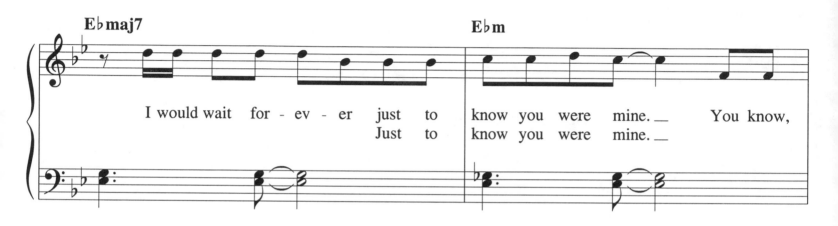

CODA

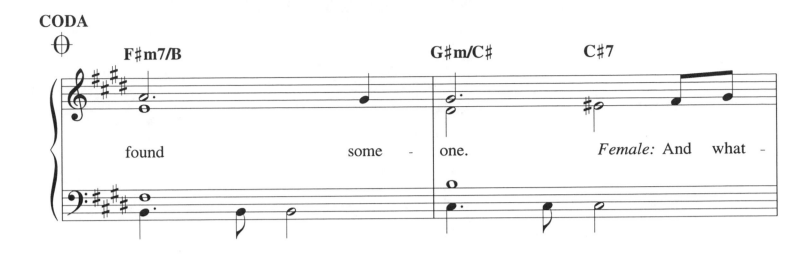

found some-one. *Female:* And what-

ev-er I do, ___ *Male:* it's just got to be you. ___ *Female:* My

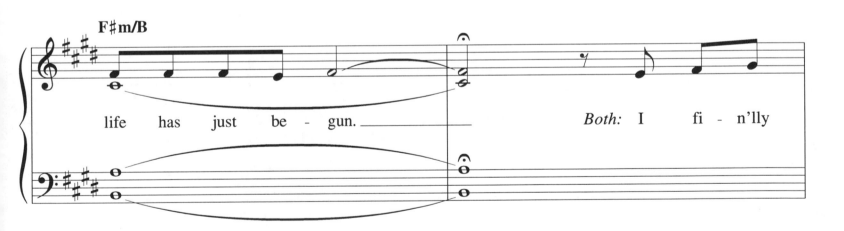

life has just be-gun. ___ *Both:* I fi-n'lly

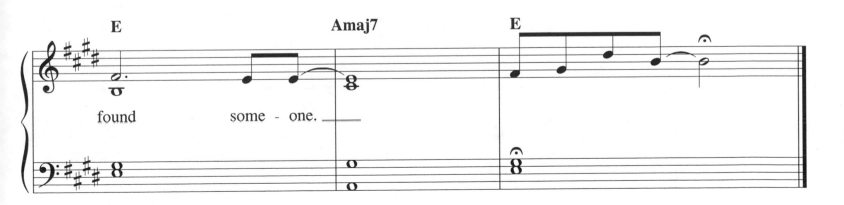

found some-one. ___

I'LL MAKE LOVE TO YOU

Words and Music by
BABYFACE

wine, ___ light the fire. _____ Girl, your wish is my com -
clothes _ on the floor _____ I'm gonna take my clothes off

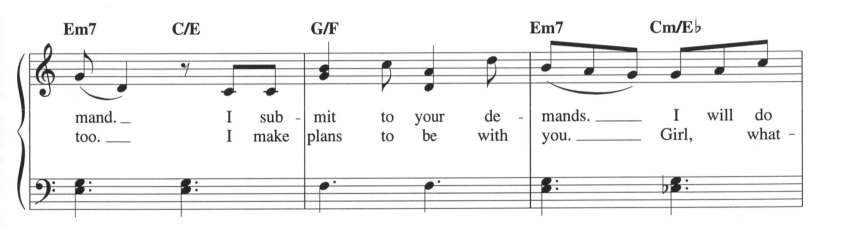

mand. _ I sub - mit to your de - mands. _____ I will do
too. _ I make plans to be with you. _____ Girl, what -

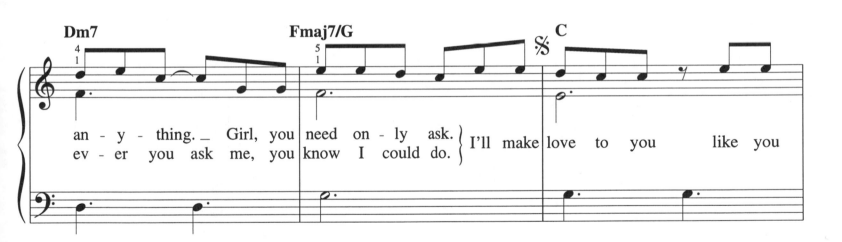

an - y - thing. _ Girl, you need on - ly ask. } I'll make love to you like you
ev - er you ask me, you know I could do.

want me to and I'll hold you tight, ba - by, all through the night, I'll make

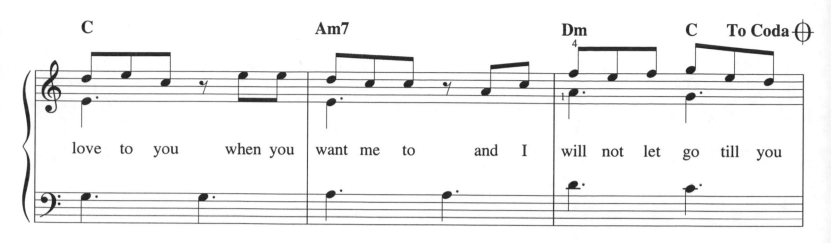

love to you   when you   want me to   and I   will not let go till you

tell me to. _____   Girl, re -   tell me to. Ba - by, to -

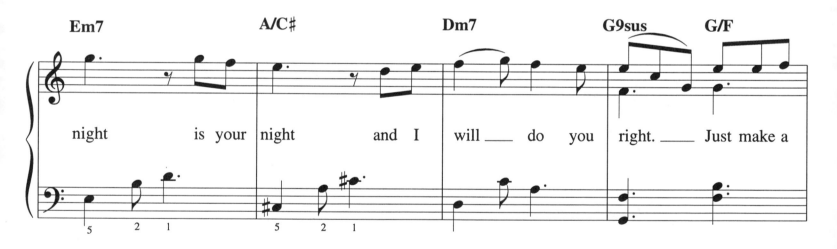

night   is your night   and I   will ___ do you   right. ___ Just make a

wish   on your night,   an - y - thing that you ask. I will   give you the love of your

IMAGINE

Words and Music by
JOHN LENNON

IT'S ALL COMING BACK TO ME NOW

Words and Music by
JIM STEINMAN

Moderately, with feeling

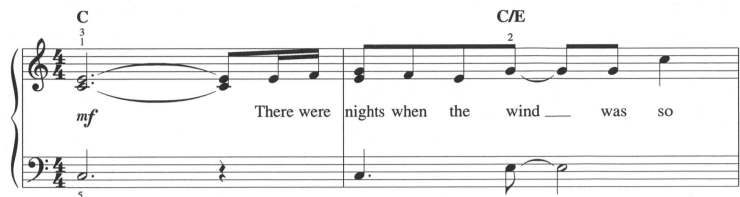

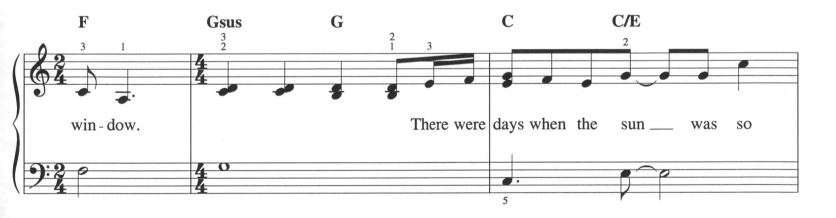

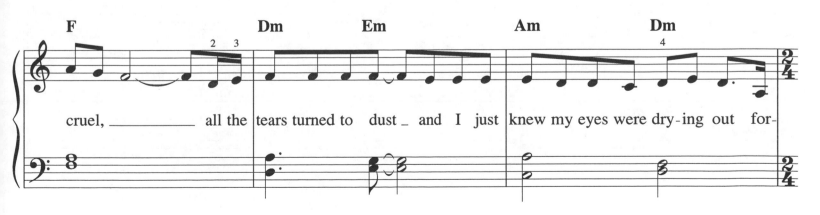

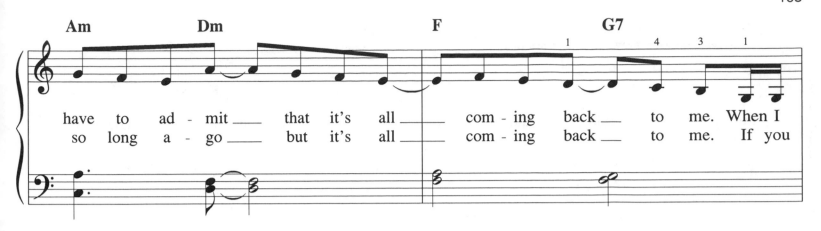

have to ad - mit ___ that it's all ___ com - ing back ___ to me. When I
so long a - go ___ but it's all ___ com - ing back ___ to me. If you

touch you like this, ___ and I hold you like that, ___ it's so
touch me like this, ___ and if I kiss you like that, ___ it was

hard to be - lieve, ___ but it's all ___ com - ing back ___ to me. It's
gone with the wind, ___ but it's all ___ com - ing back ___ to me. It's

all com - ing back, ___ it's all com - ing back to me now. ___ There were

mo - ments of gold ___ and there were flash - es of light. ___ There were

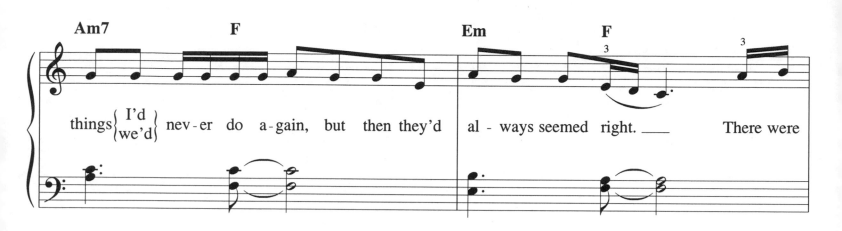

things {I'd / we'd} nev - er do a - gain, but then they'd al - ways seemed right. ___ There were

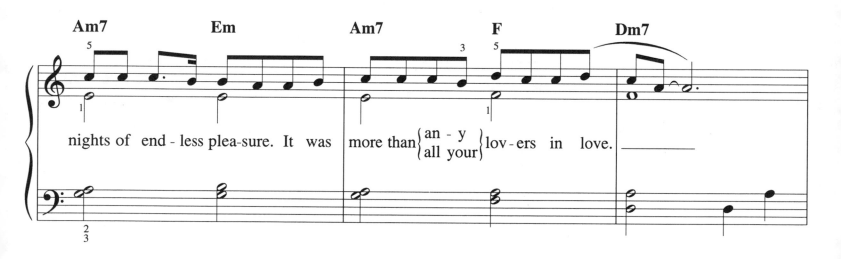

nights of end - less plea - sure. It was more than {an - y / all your} lov - ers in love. ___

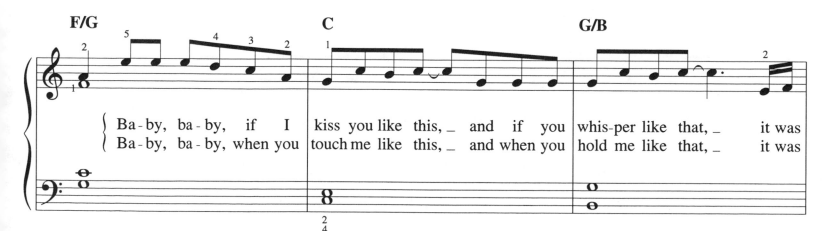

Ba - by, ba - by, if I kiss you like this, _ and if you whis - per like that, _ it was
Ba - by, ba - by, when you touch me like this, _ and when you hold me like that, _ it was

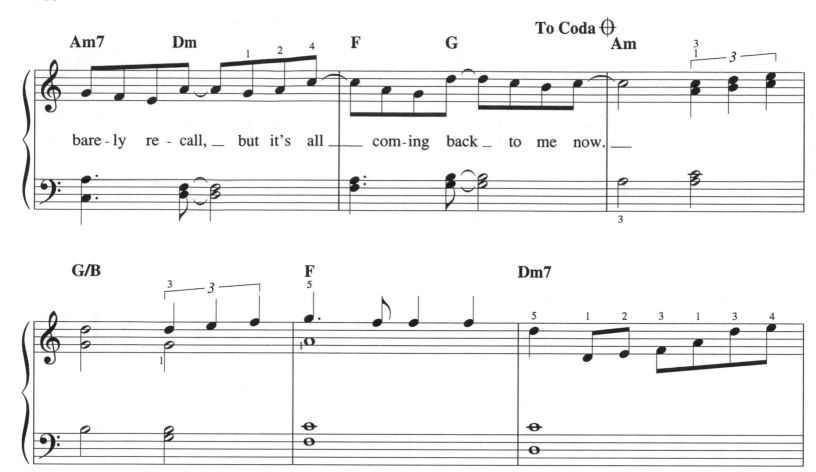

bare - ly re - call, __ but it's all __ com-ing back __ to me now. __

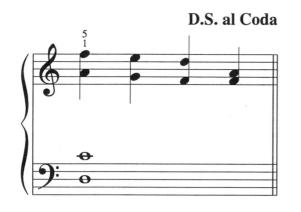

If you for -

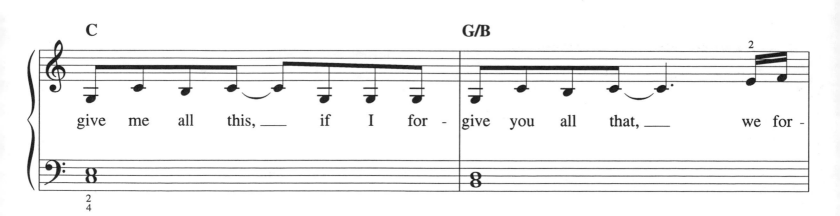

give me all this, __ if I for - give you all that, __ we for -

give and for - get, __ and it's all __ com-ing back __ to me now. It's all com-ing

back to me now. _____ And when I touch you like that, __ it's all com-ing

back to me now. _____ And if you do it like this, __ it's all com-ing

back to me now. _____ And if we...

rit.

THEME FROM "JURASSIC PARK"

from the Universal Motion Picture JURASSIC PARK

Composed by
JOHN WILLIAMS

MCA Music Publishing

THE KEEPER OF THE STARS

Words and Music by KAREN STALEY,
DANNY MAYO and DICKEY LEE

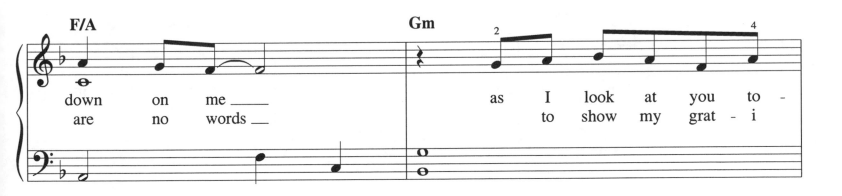

to the Keep-er of the Stars. He sure knew what he was

do - in' ___ when he joined these two hearts.

I hold ev-'ry-thing when I hold you in my

arms. I've got all I'll ev-er need,

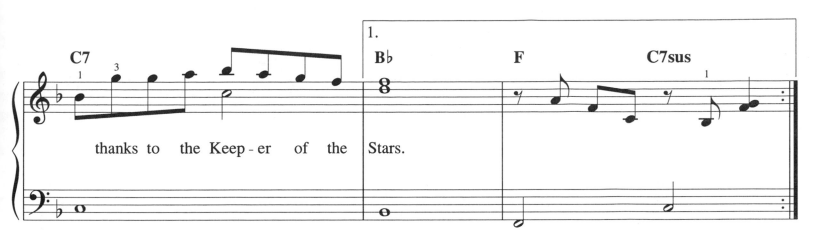

thanks to the Keep - er of the Stars.

Stars.   It   was   no

ac - ci - dent,   me find-ing you.   Some-one had a

hand   in   it ___   long be-fore we ev - er knew.

rit. e dim.

MY HEART WILL GO ON
(Love Theme from 'Titanic')
from the Paramount and Twentieth Century Fox Motion Picture TITANIC

Music by JAMES HORNER
Lyric by WILL JENNINGS

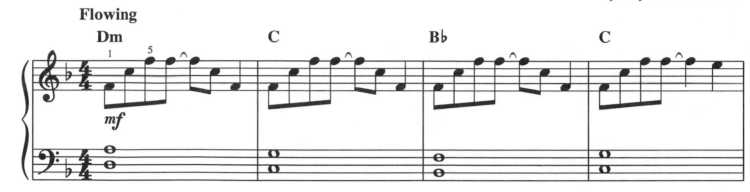

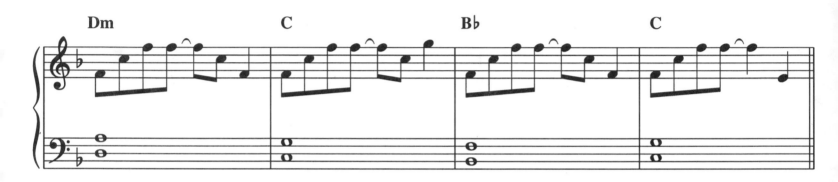

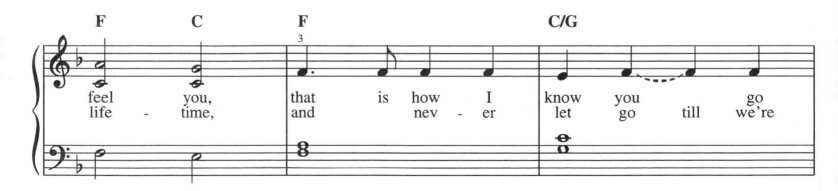

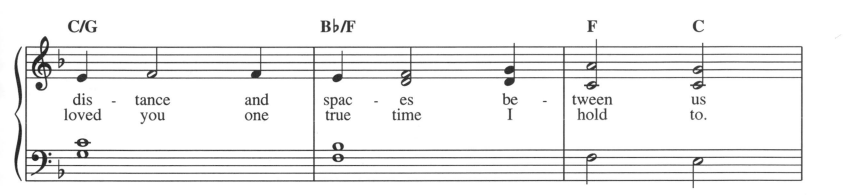

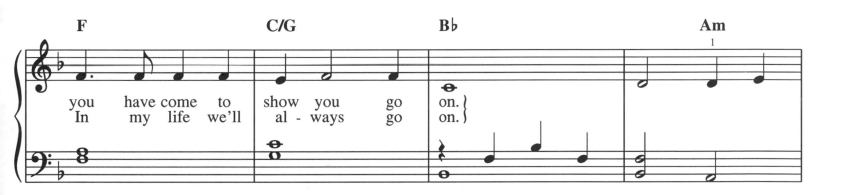

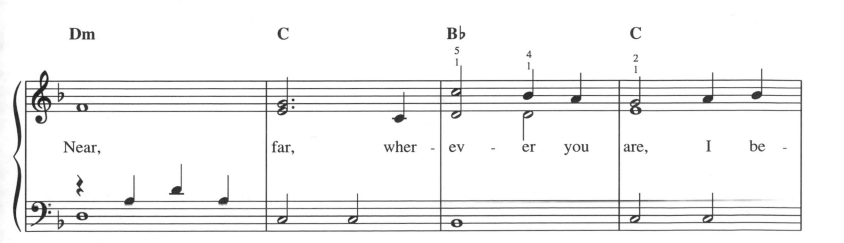

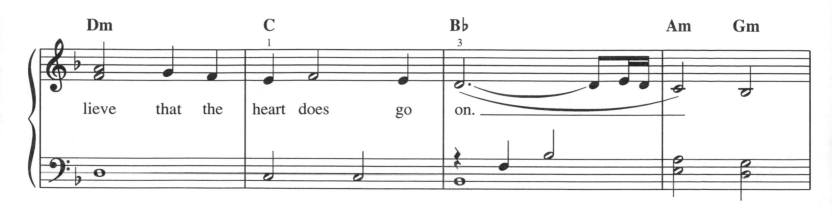

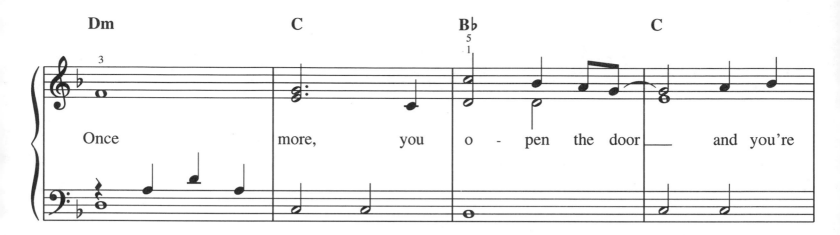

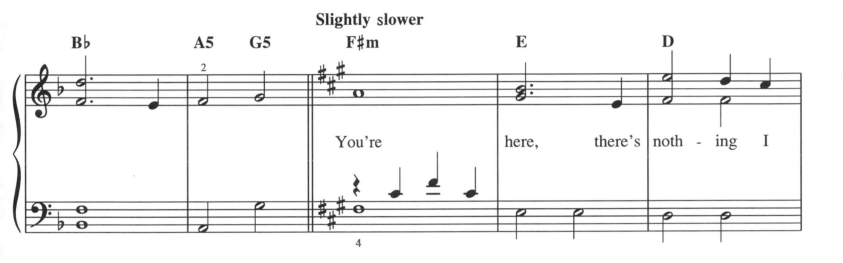

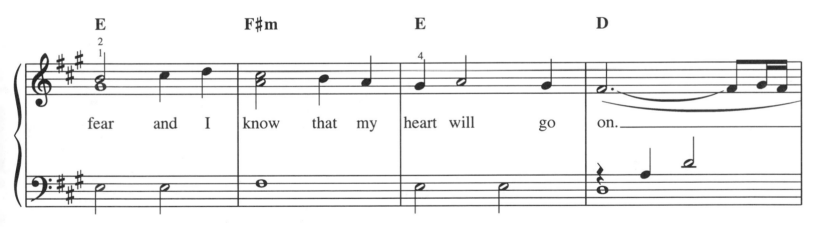

118

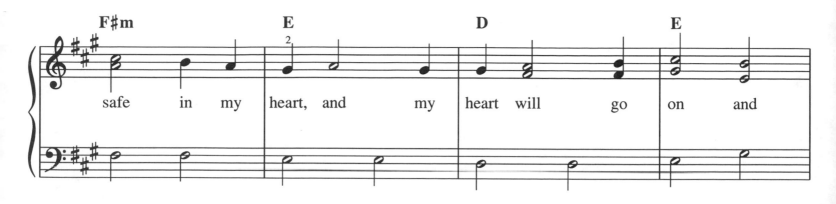

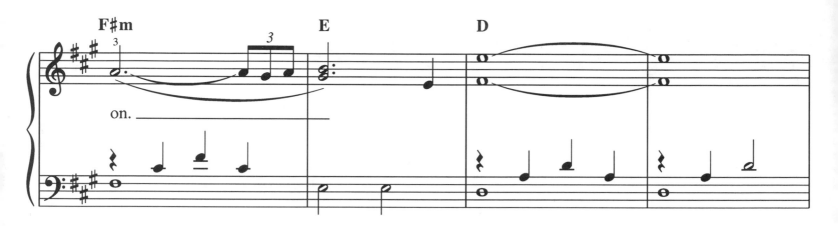

safe in my heart, and my heart will go on and

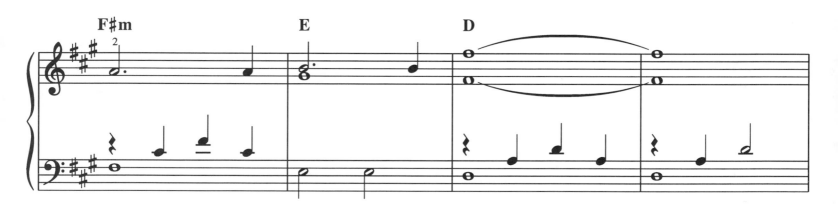

on.

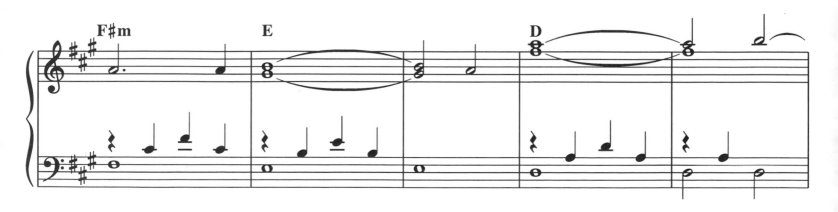

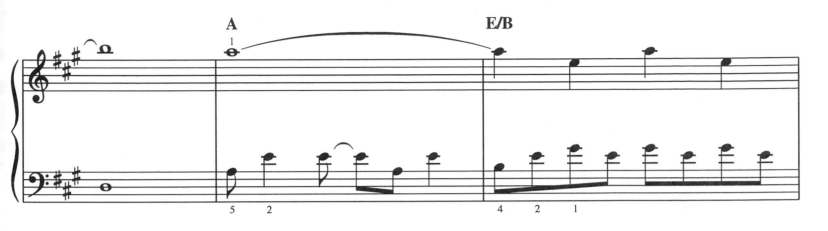

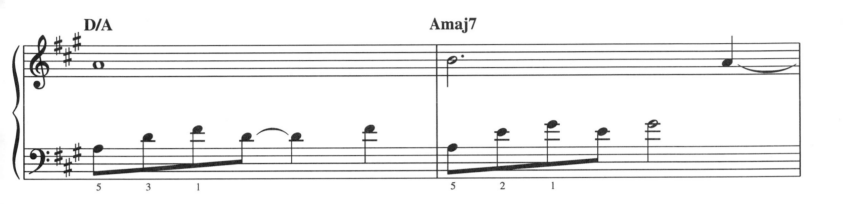

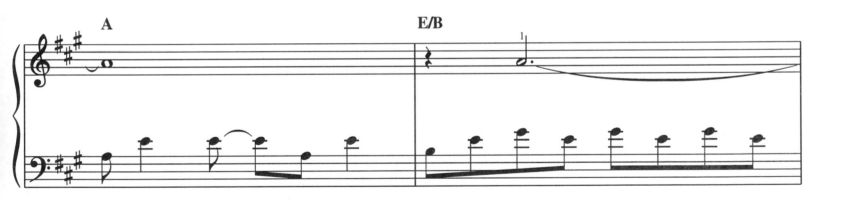

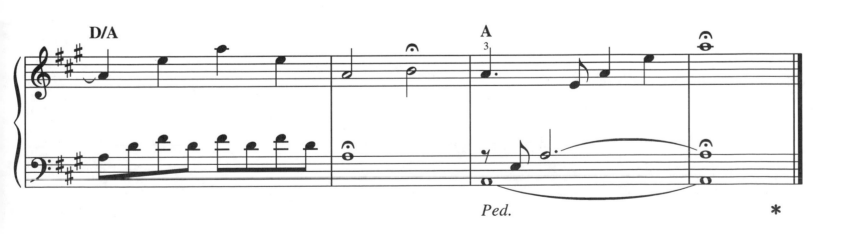

ONE SWEET DAY

Words and Music by MARIAH CAREY, WALTER AFANASIEFF, SHAWN STOCKMAN,
MICHAEL McCARY, NATHAN MORRIS and WANYA MORRIS

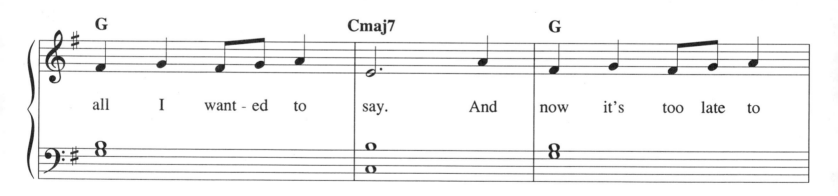

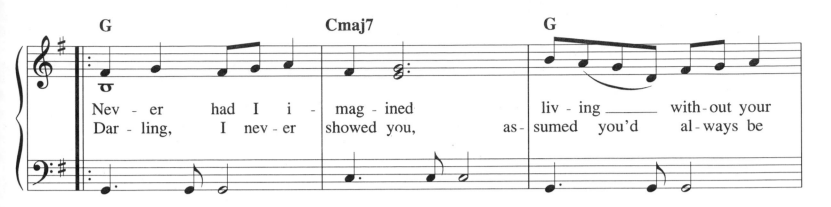

man - y friends we've lost a - long the way. ___ And I

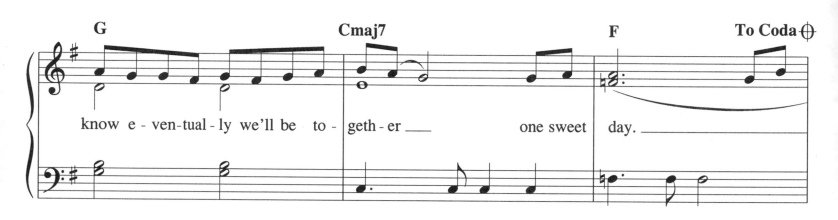

know e - ven-tual - ly we'll be to - geth - er ___ one sweet day. ___

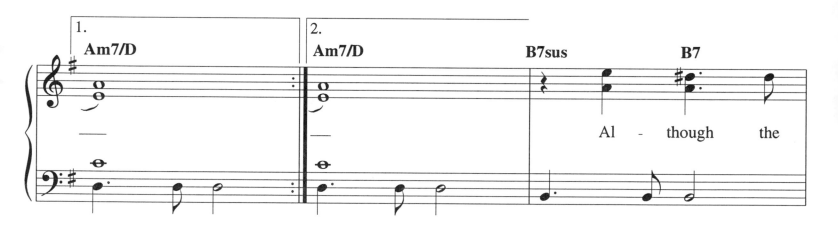

___ ___ Al - though the

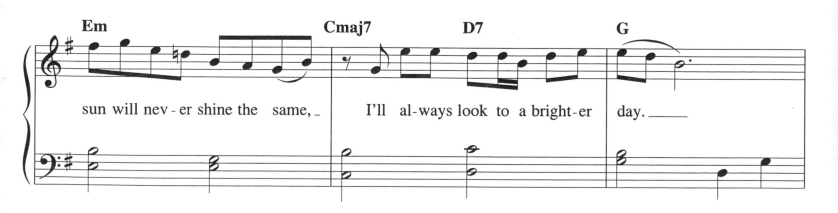

sun will nev - er shine the same, ___ I'll al-ways look to a bright-er day. ___

Lord, I ____ know when I lay me down to sleep, __

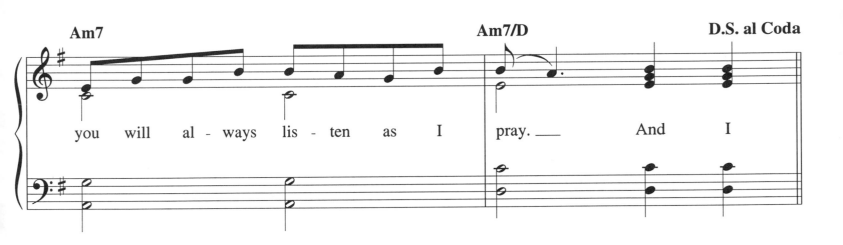

you will al - ways lis - ten as I pray. __ And I

Sor - ry I nev - er

told you all I want - ed to say.

THE POWER OF LOVE

Words by MARY SUSAN APPLEGATE and JENNIFER RUSH
Music by CANDY DEROUGE and GUNTHER MENDE

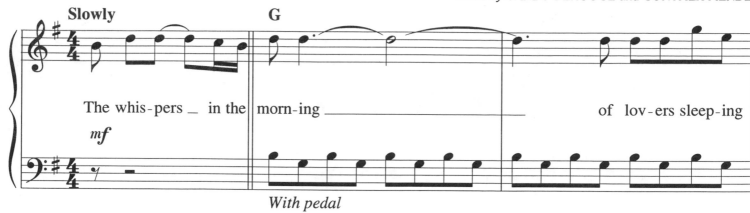

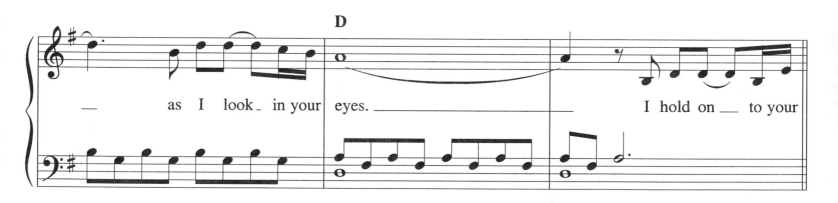

'bout the pow - er of love.

The sound of your heart

beat - ing

made it clear sud - den -

ly.

The feel - ing that I

SAVE THE BEST FOR LAST

Words and Music by PHIL GALDSTON,
JON LIND and WENDY WALDMAN

Some-times the snow comes down_ in June. Some-times the
nights you came_ to me when some sil-ly
snow comes down_ in June. Some-times the

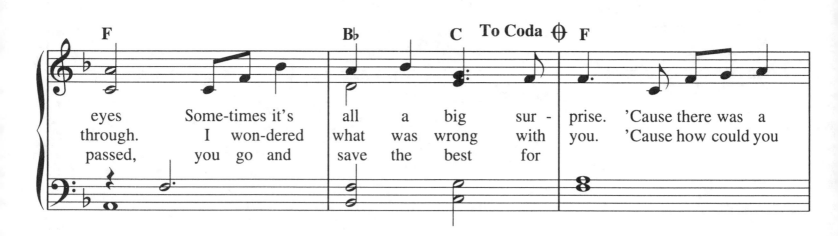

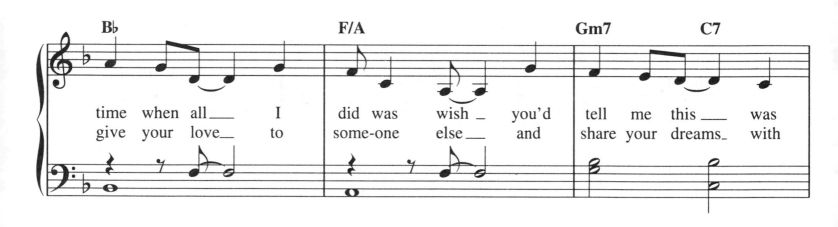

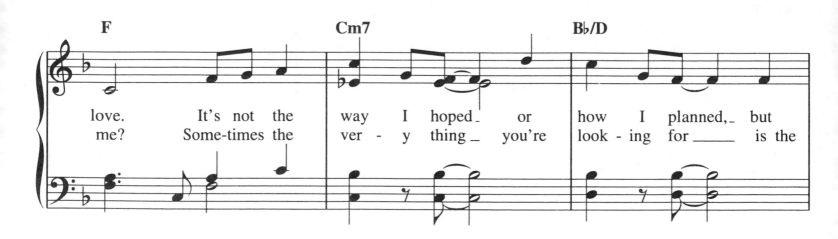

some-how it's e - nough. And now we're stand - ing face _ to
one thing you can't see. But now we're stand - ing face _ to

face.
face.
Is - n't this world a cra - zy place? Just when I

thought our chance _ had passed, you go and save the best for

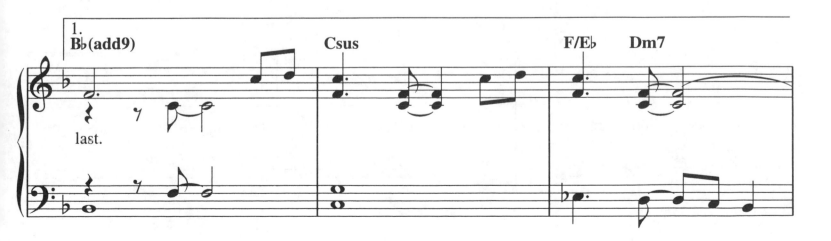

last.

All of the last.

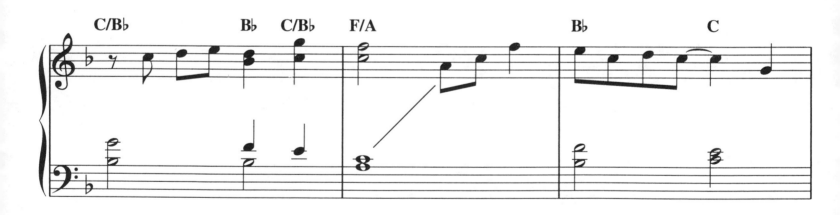

Some-times the ver - y thing _ you're look - ing for _ is the

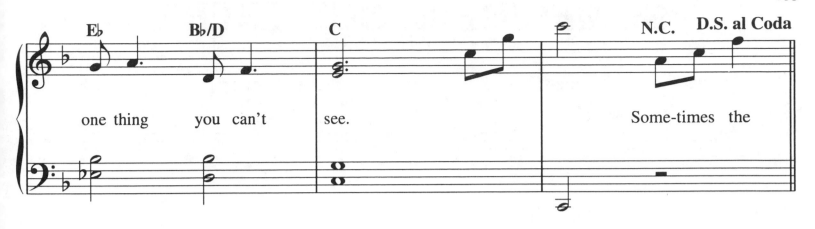

one thing   you can't   see.   Some-times the

last.

You went / and   saved the   best   for   last.

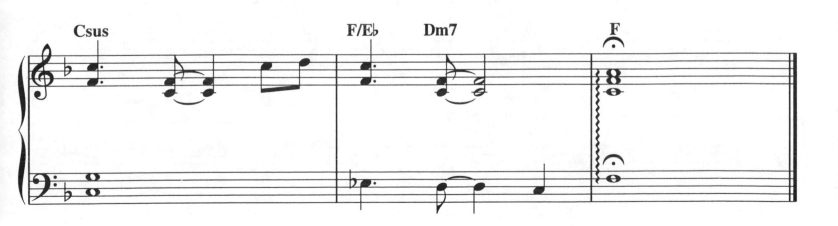

SOMEWHERE OUT THERE
from AN AMERICAN TAIL

Words and Music by JAMES HORNER,
BARRY MANN and CYNTHIA WEIL

MCA Music Publishing

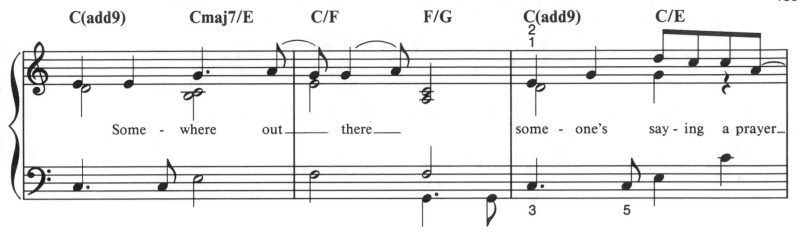

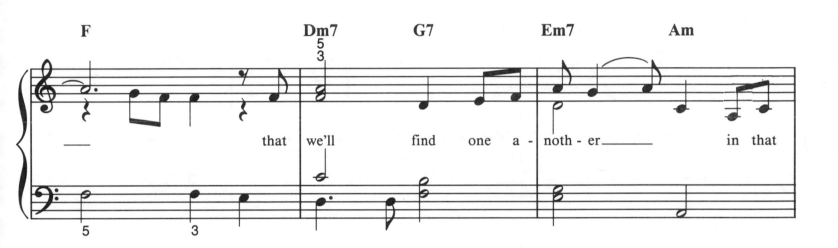

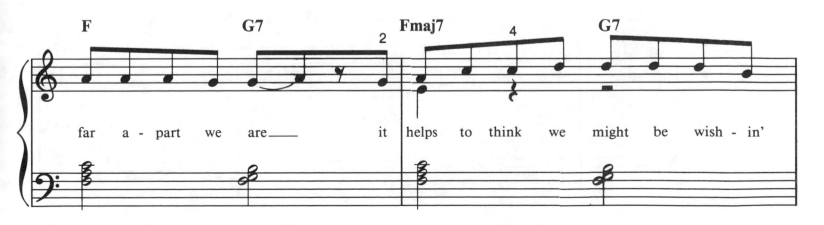

on the same bright star. And when the night wind starts to sing a -

lone-some lul-la-by it helps to think we're sleep-ing un-der - neath the same big

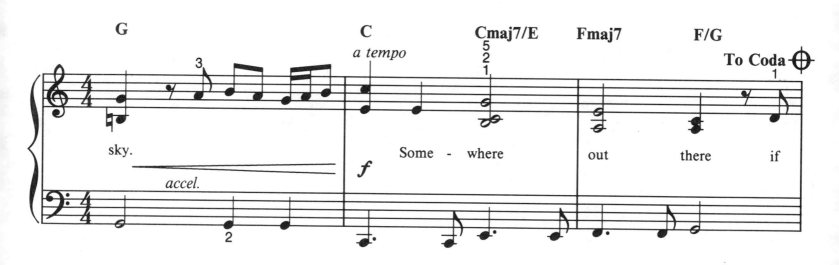

sky. Some - where out there if

love can see us through, then we'll be to - geth - er some-where

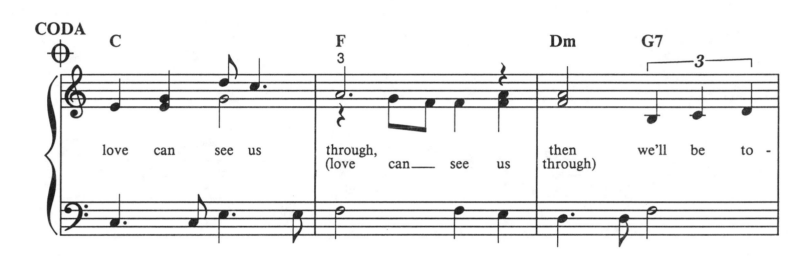

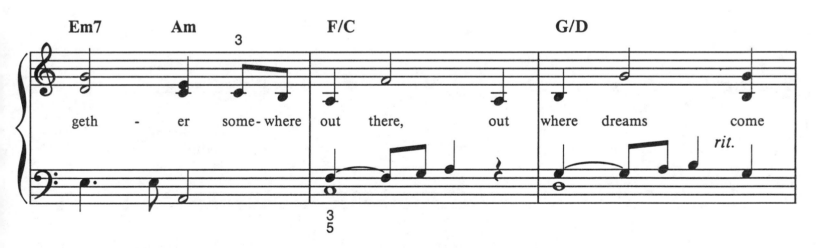

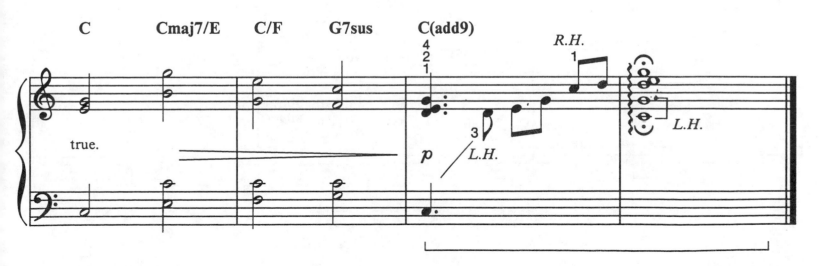

TEARS IN HEAVEN

Words and Music by ERIC CLAPTON
and WILL JENNINGS

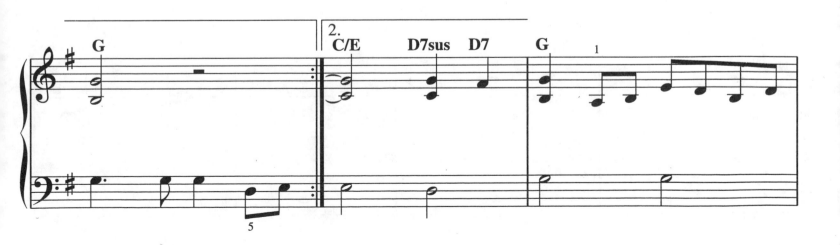

Time can bring you down,____ time can bend your knees.____

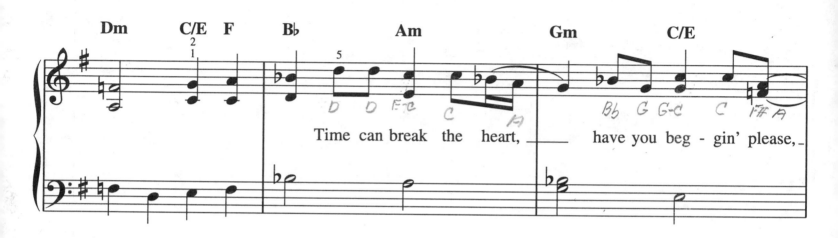

Time can break the heart,____ have you beg - gin' please,__

beg - gin' please.__ (Instrumental)

Be-yond the door

there's peace, I'm sure.___ And I know

D.S. al Coda

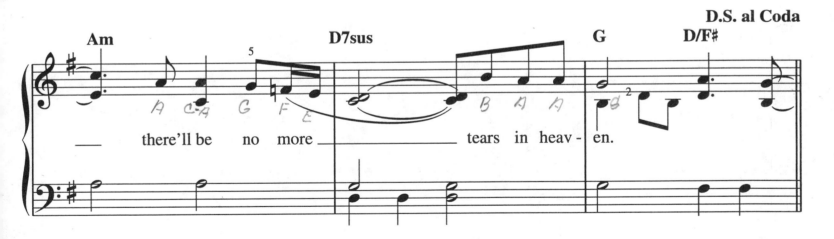

there'll be no more___ tears in heav - en.

CODA

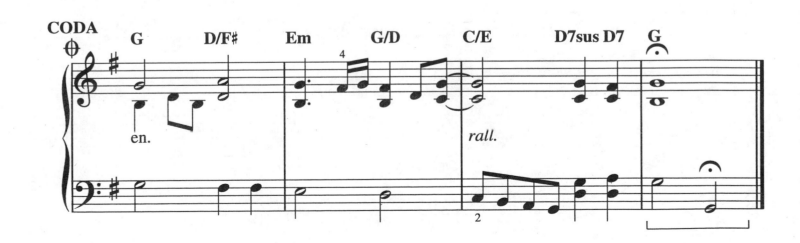

en.

rall.

VALENTINE

Words and Music by JACK KUGELL
and JIM BRICKMAN

Moderately, with expression

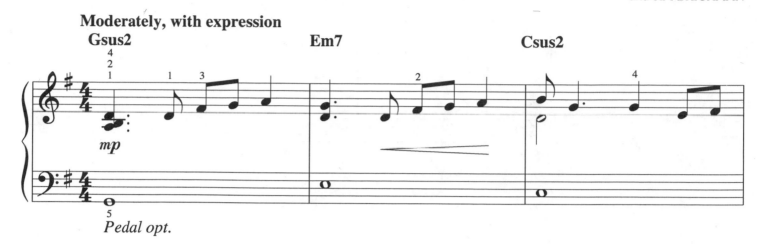

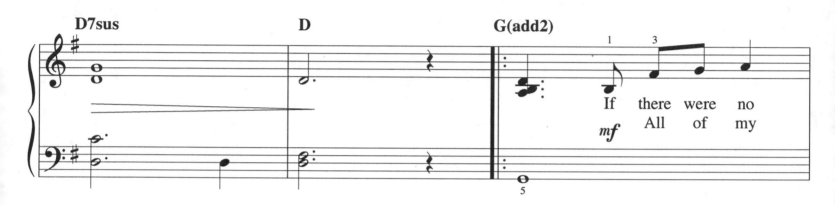

If there were no
All of my

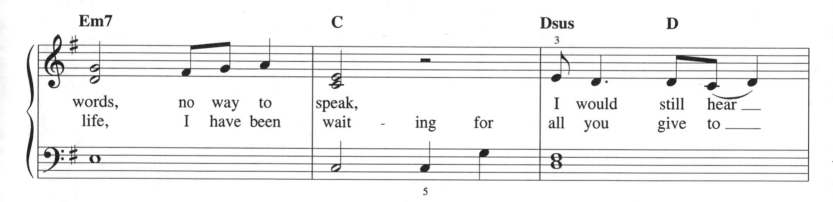

words, no way to speak, I would still hear ___
life, I have been wait - ing for all you give to ___

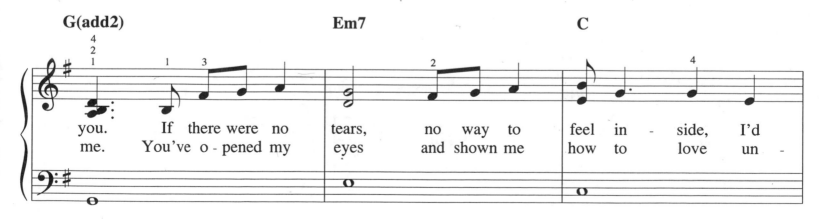

you. If there were no tears, no way to feel in - side, I'd
me. You've o - pened my eyes and shown me how to love un -

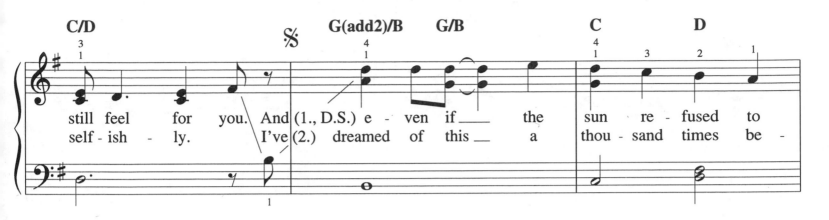

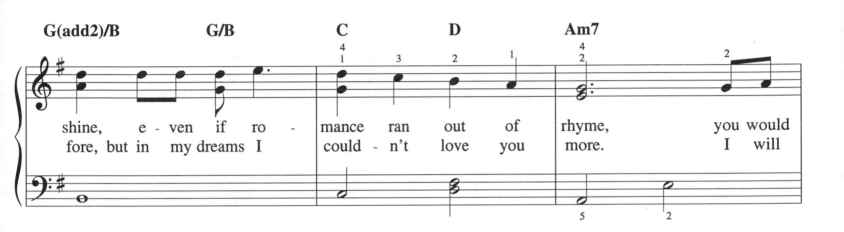

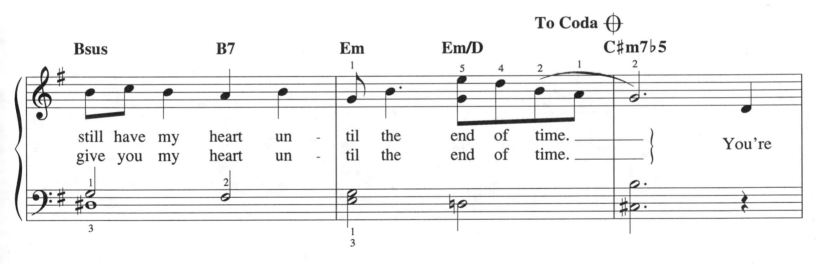

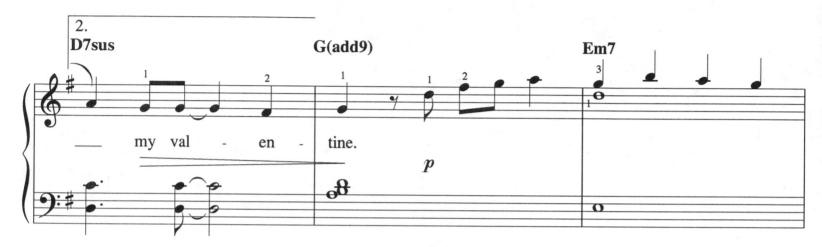

my val - en - tine.

La, la, la, la, la, _____ la. _____

And

CODA

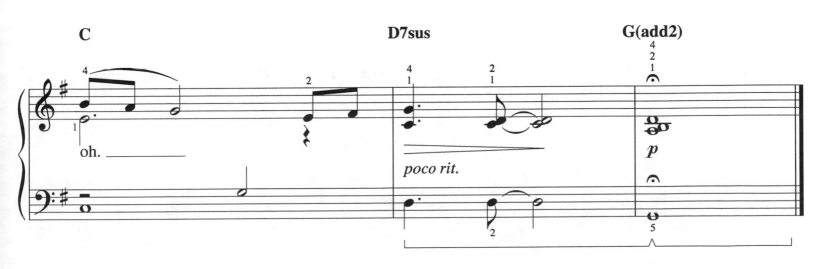

WHEN I FALL IN LOVE

featured in the TriStar Motion Picture SLEEPLESS IN SEATTLE

Words by EDWARD HEYMAN
Music by VICTOR YOUNG

rest - less world _ like this is, _____ love is end - ed _ be - fore it's _ be -

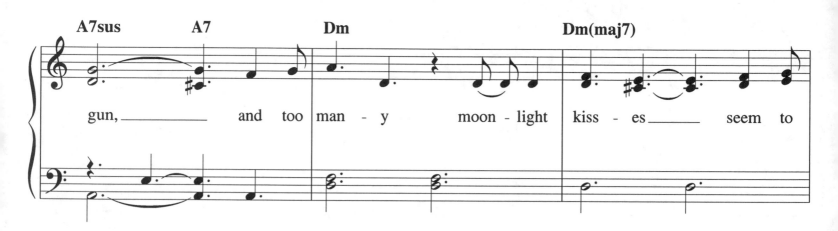

gun, _____ and too man - y moon - light kiss - es _____ seem to

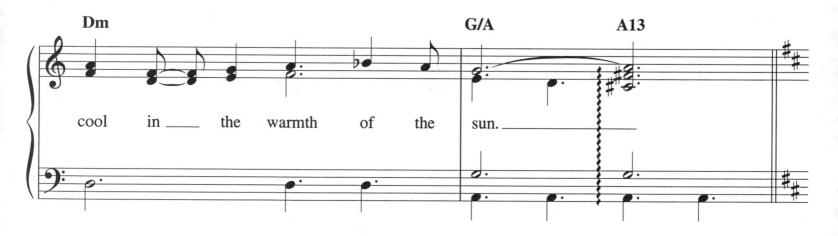

cool in _____ the warmth of the sun. _____

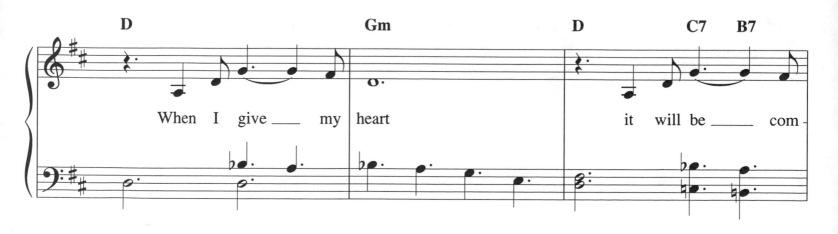

When I give ___ my heart   it will be _____ com -

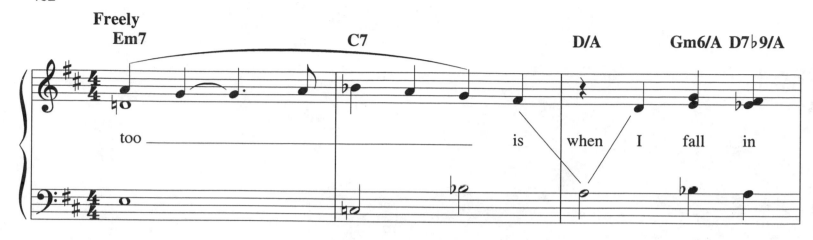

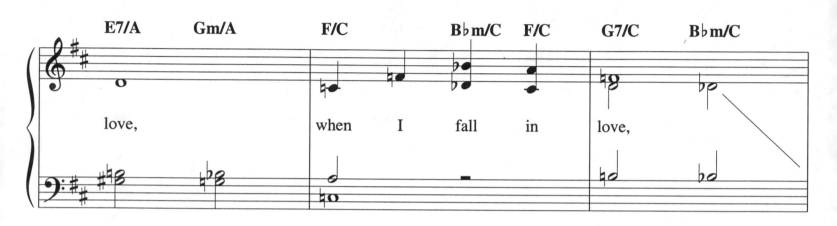

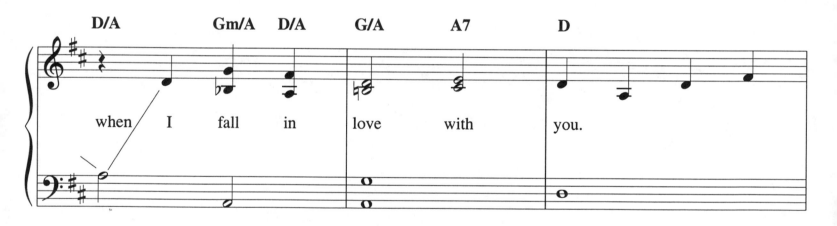

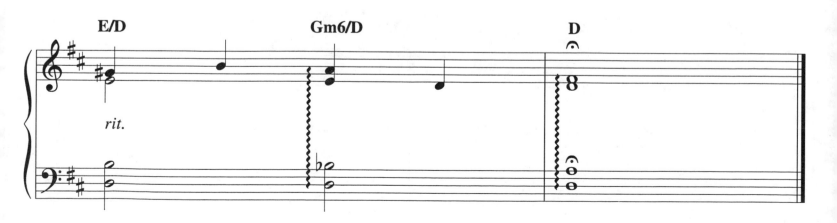

YOU MUST LOVE ME

from the Cinergi Motion Picture EVITA

Words by TIM RICE
Music by ANDREW LLOYD WEBBER

Cer - tain - ties dis - ap - pear. What do we do ___ for our

dream to sur - vive, how do we keep ___ all our pas - sions a - live as

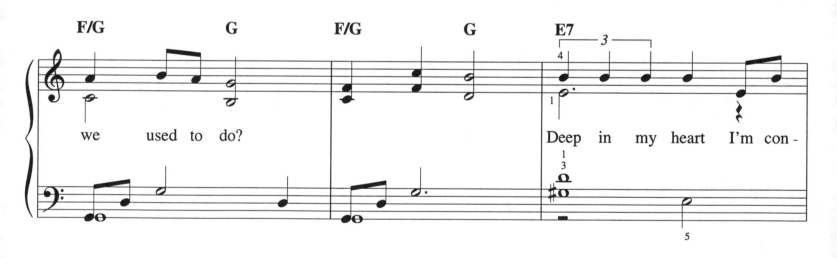

we used to do? Deep in my heart I'm con -

ceal - ing things that I'm long - ing to say,

Additional Lyrics

Verse 2: *(Instrumental 8 bars)*
Why are you at my side?
How can I be any use to you now?
Give me a chance and I'll let you see how
Nothing has changed.
Deep in my heart I'm concealing
Things that I'm longing to say,
Scared to confess what I'm feeling
Frightened you'll slip away,
You must love me.

WHEN YOU SAY NOTHING AT ALL

Words and Music by DON SCHLITZ
and PAUL OVERSTREET

Moderately slow

With pedal

It's a - maz - ing how you
All day long__ I can hear

can speak right__ to my heart.__
peo - ple talk - ing out loud.__

With - out say - ing a word__ you can light up the dark.__
But when you__ hold me near__ you drown out the crowd.__

Try as I may___ I could nev-
Old Mis-ter Web - ster could nev-

- er ex - plain___ what I hear___ when you don't___ say a thing.
- er de - fine___ what's be - ing said___ be-tween your___ heart and mine.

The smile on your face lets me know

___ that you need___ me. There's a truth in your eyes say - ing you'll

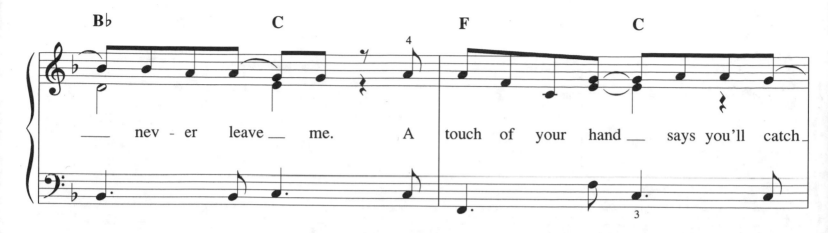

_____ nev - er leave ___ me.   A   touch of your hand ___ says you'll catch

_____ me if ev - er I fall. ___   Now

you say it best ___   when you say noth-ing at all. ___

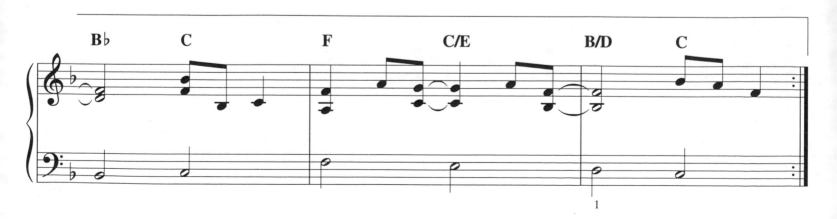

159

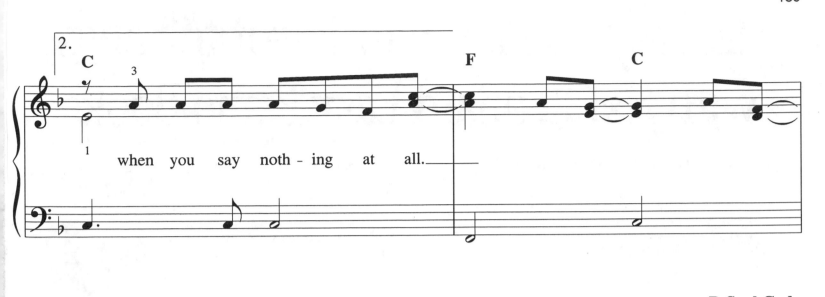

when you say noth-ing at all.

D.S. al Coda

The

CODA

when you say noth-ing at all.

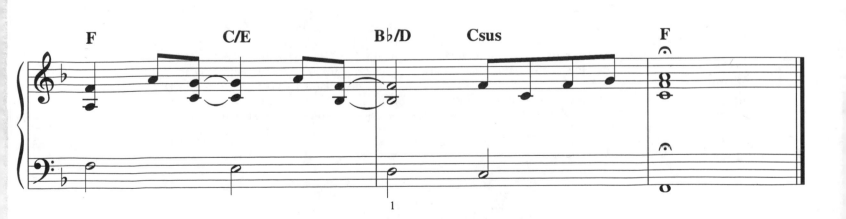

It's Easy To Play Your Favorite Songs with Hal Leonard Easy Piano Books

The Best of Today's Movie Hits
16 contemporary film favorites: Change The World • Colors Of The Wind • I Believe In You And Me • I Finally Found Someone • If I Had Words • Mission: Impossible Theme • When I Fall In Love • You Must Love Me • more.
00310248 ....$9.95

Playing The Blues
Over 30 great blues tunes arranged for easy piano: Baby, Won't You Please Come Home • Chicago Blues • Fine And Mellow • Heartbreak Hotel • Pinetop's Blues • St. Louis Blues • The Thrill Is Gone • more.
00310102 ....$12.95

The Best Songs Ever - 3rd Edition
A prestigious collection of 80 all-time favorite songs, featuring: All I Ask Of You • Beauty and the Beast • Body And Soul • Candle In The Wind • Crazy • Don't Know Much • Endless Love • Fly Me To The Moon • The Girl From Ipanema • Here's That Rainy Day • Imagine • In The Mood • Let It Be • Longer • Moonlight In Vermont • People • Satin Doll • Save The Best For Last • Somewhere Out There • Stormy Weather • Strangers In The Night • Tears In Heaven • What A Wonderful World • When I Fall In Love • and more
00359223 ....$19.95

Country Love Songs
34 classic and contemporary country favorites, including: The Dance • A Few Good Things Remain • Forever And Ever Amen • I Never Knew Love • Love Can Build A Bridge • Love Without End, Amen • She Believes In Me • She Is His Only Need • Where've You Been • and more.
00110030 ....$12.95

R&B Love songs
27 songs, including: Ain't Nothing Like The Real Thing • Easy • Exhale (Shoop Shoop) • The First Time Ever I Saw Your Face • Here And Now • I'm Your Baby Tonight • My Girl • Never Can Say Goodbye • Ooo Baby Baby • Save The Best For Last • Someday • Still • and more.
00310181 ....$12.95

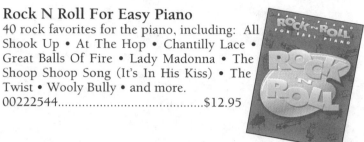

Rock N Roll For Easy Piano
40 rock favorites for the piano, including: All Shook Up • At The Hop • Chantilly Lace • Great Balls Of Fire • Lady Madonna • The Shoop Shoop Song (It's In His Kiss) • The Twist • Wooly Bully • and more.
00222544 ....$12.95

I'll Be Seeing You
50 Songs Of World War II
A salute to the music and memories of WWII, including a chronology of events on the homefront, dozens of photos, and 50 radio favorites of the GIs and their families back home. Includes: Boogie Woogie Bugle Boy • Don't Sit Under The Apple Tree (With Anyone Else But Me) • I Don't Want To Walk Without You • Moonlight In Vermont • and more.
00310147 ....$17.95

Disney's The Hunchback Of Notre Dame Selections
10 selections from Disney's animated classic, complete with beautiful color illustrations. Includes: The Bells Of Notre Dame • God Help The Outcasts • Out There • Someday • and more.
00316011 ....$14.95

Today's Love Songs
31 contemporary favorites, including: All I Ask Of You • Because I Love You • Don't Know Much • Endless Love • Forever And Ever, Amen • Here And Now • I'll Be Loving You Forever • Lost In Your Eyes • Love Without End, Amen • Rhythm Of My Heart • Unchained Melody • Vision Of Love • and more.
00222541 ....$14.95

Best Of Cole Porter
Over 30 songs, including: Be A Clown • Begin The Beguine • Easy To Love • From This Moment On • In The Still Of The Night • Night And Day • So In Love • Too Darn Hot • You Do Something To Me • You'd Be So Nice To Come Home To • and more
00311576 ....$14.95

FOR MORE INFORMATION, SEE YOUR LOCAL MUSIC DEALER, OR WRITE TO:

HAL•LEONARD® CORPORATION
7777 W. BLUEMOUND RD. P.O. BOX 13819 MILWAUKEE, WI 53213

Prices, book contents, and availability subject to change without notice

0597